RELIGION IN THE POPULAR PRINTS 1600-1832

Series Editor: Michael Duffy

The other titles in this series are:

The Common People and Politics 1750–1790s *by John Brewer*
Caricatures and the Constitution 1760–1832 *by H.T. Dickinson*
The Englishman and the Foreigner *by Michael Duffy*
Walpole and the Robinocracy *by Paul Langford*
Crime and the Law in English Satirical Prints 1600–1832 *by J.A. Sharpe*
The American Revolution *by Peter D.G. Thomas*

THE ENGLISH SATIRICAL PRINT 1600-1832

Religion in the Popular Prints 1600-1832

by John Miller

CHADWYCK-HEALEY

CAMBRIDGE

© 1986 Chadwyck-Healey Ltd

All rights reserved. No part of this work may be reproduced, stored in a retrieval system, or transmitted in any form, or by any means, electronic, mechanical, photocopying, recording or otherwise, without written permission from Chadwyck-Healey Ltd.

First published 1986

ISBN 0 85964 170 8

Chadwyck-Healey Ltd.
Cambridge Place, Cambridge CB2 1NR England

Chadwyck-Healey Inc.
1021 Prince Street, Alexandria, VA 22314 USA

British Library Cataloguing in Publication Data

Miller, John
   Religion in the popular prints, 1600–1832.—
   (The English satirical print, 1600–1832)
    1. Prints, English 2. Satire, English—History and criticism 3. Religion in art
   I. Title II. Series
   769′,48   NE958.3.G7

Library of Congress Cataloging in Publication Data

Miller, John
   Religion in the popular prints, 1600–1832.

   (The English satirical print, 1600––1832)
   Bibliography: p.
    1. English wit and humor, Pictorial. 2. Religion—Caricatures and cartoons. I. Title II. Series.
   NC1473.M55   1985   769.942   85-5938

Printed by Unwin Brothers Limited, Old Woking, Surrey

CONTENTS

Publisher's Note	7
General Editor's Preface	9
Preface	11
Introduction	13
The Seventeenth Century, 1603–1714	15
The Eighteenth Century, 1714–*c.*1780	31
The Age of Reform, *c.*1780–1832	43
Footnotes	55
The Plates	61

PUBLISHER'S NOTE

In 1978 Chadwyck-Healey published *English Cartoons and Satirical Prints 1320-1832 in the British Museum* in which the 17,000 prints listed in the *Catalogue of Political and Personal Satires* by F. G. Stephens and M. D. George are reproduced on microfilm identified by their catalogue numbers.

British Museum Publications reprinted the Stephens and George catalogue to accompany the microfilm edition and for the first time it became possible for scholars to study the prints that are so exhaustively described in Stephens and George, without needing to visit the Department of Prints and Drawings.

It also made this series possible for it is doubtful whether the seven authors would ever have been able to spend the time in the British Museum necessary to search through this huge collection. As it was they each had access to the microfilm edition which they used for their research.

The reprint of the Stephens and George catalogue is itself now out of print but has been reissued on microfilm by Chadwyck-Healey.

GENERAL EDITOR'S PREFACE

In the course of the seventeenth and eighteenth centuries the English satirical print emerged as a potent vehicle for the expression of political and social opinion. Their development was slow at first, but picking up pace from the 1720s, the prints stood out by the 1780s as the most striking symbol of the freedom of the press in England. Sold usually individually, as works of art as well as of polemic, by the late eighteenth century they constituted the basis of a thriving commercial industry and had established themselves as one of the predominant art forms of the age. The graphic skill of the engraver as well as the pungency of his message makes the English satirical print an immensely attractive, entertaining and very fruitful source for the study of Stuart and Hanoverian England. Surprisingly, although many of the prints survive, this source has been frequently neglected, and it is the aim of this series to remedy that deficiency by showing through the study of selected aspects of the period between 1600 and 1832 how the historian can illuminate the prints and prints can illuminate history. All art forms are the product of particular political and social environments, and this volume together with the rest of the series hopes to set this particular art form – the English satirical print – in its proper historical context by revealing how it gave graphic representation to the ideas, assumptions and environment of that era.

Michael Duffy

PREFACE

The purpose of this volume is to offer a selection of the prints on religious topics produced between 1600 and 1832 and to place them in their historical context. It does not purport to offer a general history of caricature, for which the reader is referred to M. D. George, *English Political Caricature: A Study of Opinion and Propaganda* (2 vols., Oxford, 1959). Nor does it provide a detailed analysis of each print, for that can be found in F. G. Stephens and M. D. George, *Catalogue of the Prints and Drawings in the British Museum* (11 vols., London, 1870–1954). All the prints are taken from the collection of personal and political satires in the British Museum. Each is marked with its number in that collection, with the abbreviation BMC. The numbers in italics in the text refer to the prints in this volume.

   I should like to thank the series editor, Michael Duffy, for his help in preparing this volume and my colleague, Michael Port, for reading and commenting on the introduction. Any errors which remain are, of course, my own.

Queen Mary College, London   *John Miller*
July 1980

INTRODUCTION

Between James I's accession and the passing of the Great Reform Bill England underwent changes far more profound and extensive than had occurred over the previous five centuries. Industrialisation and urbanisation were transforming the economy and society, while in politics the landed elite, having stripped the monarch of effective authority, faced insistent demands that it should share its power with other social groups. The changes in the nation's religious life were no less complex. In 1603 almost nobody questioned the need for a single national church, to which all should conform on pain of punishment, although there were disagreements about the form it should take. By 1832 there was a bewildering variety of denominations whose members enjoyed religious liberty and full political rights. The developments of the intervening period owed much to the internal dynamics of the various churches, to politics and personalities, but also to the changing social and political context within which the churches operated and to changing attitudes to God and to revealed religion. In 1603 few openly questioned the existence of God or the veracity of the Bible, although there were many (especially in remote upland areas) whose knowledge of Christianity was minimal. In time, however, scientific advances seemed, to some, to offer a different explanation of phenomena which could once be understood only as God's handiwork and to cast doubt on the credibility of some parts of the Bible. Thus alongside denominational bickerings and arguments about the churches' political views and pastoral failings, there were some who doubted whether churches were necessary at all.

The purpose of this introduction is to consider how far and how accurately religious developments were reflected in the popular prints. One would not expect the reflection to be wholly precise, for several reasons. First, there were government restrictions on publishing. For much of the seventeenth century the press was controlled through a system of licences: printers and publishers of unlicensed works risked severe punishment. After the last Licensing Act lapsed in 1695, authors and publishers might still be prosecuted under the libel or treason laws, although neither was used very often in the eighteenth century, as a trial gave great publicity to the offending publication. Even after the rise of political and religious radicalism, no formal censorship was introduced, although some radical authors and publishers were harassed in the law courts. In general, governments were more concerned about the written word than about cartoons and no print-makers were prosecuted.[1]

Unable to suppress oppositionist literature, ministers used subtler means, subsidising favourable propaganda and restricting the market for political publications by means of a stamp tax on printed paper. This tax accentuated the two salient features of the market for prints and satires in the eighteenth century: it was comparatively affluent and essentially metropolitan. In the 1750s a typical print might cost 6d plain and 1s coloured. By 1832 the price had probably doubled and collections like *Maclean's Monthly Sheet of Caricatures* cost several shillings. Such prices would be beyond the means of most wage-earners and craftsmen. As for the market's metropolitan bias, not one print in this collection is marked as being printed or sold in a provincial town, although one or two were produced abroad. Although provincial newspapers were developing apace, the print trade was firmly dominated by London.

The fact that eighteenth- and early nineteenth-century print-makers catered primarily for the comparatively affluent London-based market helps to explain the prints' emphases and omissions. If some had a definite polemical purpose, many sought merely to entertain or (like Gillray) could satirise all sides. Many religious prints dealt with the follies and vices of the Anglican clergy. Some satirised early London Methodists but there is almost no reference to the New Dissent and rural revivalism of the 1790s, which appealed mainly to the poor of the provinces.

The fact that print-makers produced what their customers would buy added further distortions to a medium which already showed certain limitations in dealing with religious subjects. Religious faith and experience may have inspired great art, but the purpose of satire and caricature is to deflate, not to inspire. The satirist may have a deep and serious purpose, but more often his aim is to amuse or score quick polemical points. To make those points effectively, he has to simplify, to reduce abstract concepts to concrete recognisable forms. The constant tendency towards superficiality and trivialisation is especially apparent when dealing with religion. One cannot adequately discuss such abstruse concepts as predestination in pictorial form. Moreover, some aspects of religion might seem too sacred for the mockery or frivolity of the satirist: holy communion, for example,[2] or the prayers in which the believer came face to face with God. 'Religious' prints mostly dealt not with the spiritual side of religion but with its political and social aspects – the connections of Catholicism with absolutism, the greed and idleness of the Anglican clergy, and so on. Some themes, like the drunken parson, were perennial favourites but most prints in this collection were produced on particular occasions. They might represent a sensational event (like those surrounding Joanna Southcott) but most were inspired by political crises in which religion played a part and so were intended to serve an immediate polemical purpose. Thus the prints give an incomplete and inadequate picture of religious change in this period, but they do illustrate the importance of religious issues in many political controversies.

I.
The Seventeenth Century 1603–1714

For much of this period (notably before 1640 and between 1660 and 1679) the government effectively controlled the press and few satirical prints appeared. This was one reason (though only one) for the comparatively small output of prints before 1714.[3] However, among those which appeared, religion was a far more dominant theme than was to be the case later.

1. THE ANTI-CATHOLIC HERITAGE

If one theme spanned the whole period to 1832 it was anti-Catholicism. The experience of Tudor Protestantism left a legacy of hatred of 'Popery' expressed in arguments which changed little over the next two centuries. Those arguments owed little to liturgical or theological differences or to Rome's alleged obscurantism and hostility to intellectual freedom, but concentrated mainly on the political connotations of Popery. Mary Tudor's reign was used to show that Catholic regimes persecuted Protestants with wanton cruelty (*1*).* Lay Catholics, if not themselves bloodthirsty, were manipulated by the priests who, in turn, were controlled by the pope who would use any means to advance the Catholic interest. He might declare a lawful prince deposed, but would reinforce a ruler's authority provided it was used to advance Catholicism. Thus James II was accused of seeking to establish a monarchy that was both Catholic and absolute. In Protestant states the Catholics were a dangerous 'fifth column', ready to rise up against their natural ruler at the pope's command; they could thus never be loyal to a Protestant prince. The Gunpowder Plot was merely the most spectacular of many plots against the English state (*2, 3*) and the Irish massacres of 1641 and the Great Fire (*26*) added to the list of the foul deeds attributed to the Papists. Anti-Catholicism was such a part of Protestantism that it could be turned against anyone: Methodists, Unitarians, even republican sympathisers.[4] Much anti-Popery reflected limited understanding (*145*). Defoe wrote of 'stout fellows that would spend the last drop of their blood against Popery that do not know whether it be a man or a horse'. Cobbett, when young, believed that 'the pope was a prodigious woman [the whore of Babylon] dressed in a dreadful robe which had been made red by being dipped in the blood of Protestants'.[5]

---

*Italicised numbers in the text refer to the plates in this volume. Numbers prefixed with BMC refer to catalogue numbers in the British Museum *Catalogue of Political and Personal Satires*[1]

In poking fun at the sillier manifestations of anti-Popery it is all too easy to underestimate its political importance. In the seventeenth century the struggles of Popery and Protestantism were seen in apocalyptic terms. James II's contemporaries were sure that he wished to subvert the traditional constitution and impose Popery. James's flight to France linked Catholicism even more closely with foreign conquest. After the failure of the last Jacobite rebellion in 1746, it might seem, logically, that anti-Popery should have diminished, but it did not. It had never been an entirely rational phenomenon and would not necessarily decrease in virulence merely because the English Catholics no longer seemed dangerous. Among traditionally-minded Protestants, like Wesley and Wilberforce, and among the artisans of London it remained vigorous and received a new stimulus when the Union of 1800 made the Irish Catholics' demands for emancipation a British question. English hostility to the Irish – deep, heavily mixed with contempt and sharpened by Irish immigration – added a new dimension and renewed force to anti-Popery. The priests' control over their flocks through the confessional and the Church's hostility to mixed marriages, together with the influx of Irish, reinforced the traditional view of Catholics as un-English, separate from the rest of society. A majority of British people was hostile to Catholic emancipation and each subsequent attempt to improve the position of Catholics provoked similar hostility.[6] Even now a certain residual hostility to Catholicism can be found even (perhaps especially) among those who would not regard themselves as practising Protestants.

2. THE LAUDIAN COUNTER-REFORMATION

In 1603 the Church of England was, in most respects, 'Puritan'. 'Puritanism' is not easy to define, but two definitions seem more satisfactory than most. One, 'the hotter sort of Protestants', stresses that English Puritanism was more a matter of temperament than of adherence to a particular ecclesiastical programme. The other would include all who thought the 1559 church settlement insufficiently Protestant. That settlement laid the foundations of the modern Church of England, but seemed at the time unsatisfactory and provisional. To Elizabeth, who wished to return to the marginally reformed Catholicism of her father's reign, it was too Protestant. Since Henry VIII's death, however, English Protestantism had become far more radical, so those who were to run Elizabeth's Church were much more Protestant than she was. Their dominance in the universities ensured that their views, not hers, would be passed on to new generations of ordinands. Although most Puritans had little quarrel with the doctrine and government of the Church, they resented the retention in the Prayer Book of certain Catholic practices and the queen's attempts to restrict the preaching and religious discussion which alone could bring about England's conversion to Protestantism and moral regeneration. As Elizabeth refused to change the Prayer Book service, Puritans were driven to subterfuge and deceit. Clergymen, often encouraged by their patrons and parishioners, omitted ceremonies they disliked and adapted the official service. Such conduct irritated tidy-minded bishops, but became too general to be rooted out without an unacceptable degree of disruption.[7]

James I thus inherited a Church more Protestant in practice than in theory. There was no reason why that should displease him. He was a Calvinist and an ecclesiastical politician skilful enough to reintroduce episcopacy in Scotland. Under James the English Church enjoyed something like peace until the rise of Arminianism in the 1620s.[8] Arminius had challenged the central Calvinist tenet of predestination, whereby God had long ago ordained who should be saved and who damned, irrespective of their personal conduct. Arminius's doctrines were condemned by an international Calvinist synod (to which James sent a delegation) but won a following among those of the English clergy who were reacting against the starkness of Puritanism. By the 1630s, the English Arminians, led by William Laud, controlled many of the key positions in the Church and universities and sought to impose their beliefs and practices on the nation.

Laud's regime marked a sharp reversal of the ecclesiastical trends of the reigns of Elizabeth and James. Laud even refused a licence to reprint Foxe's *Book of Martyrs*. Although predestination might seem smug and callous, condemning most people to hell-fire even before they were born, it was (to quote the Thirty-Nine Articles) 'full of sweet, pleasant and unspeakable comfort to godly persons and such as feel in themselves the working of the spirit of Christ'.[9] It had also been the accepted teaching of the Elizabethan Church. In rejecting predestination the Laudians restored to the individual a certain freedom to accept or reject the grace which God offered and so moved closer to the teachings of the Roman Church. In other ways, too, Laud sought to restore features of the pre-Reformation Church which the Puritans had sought to destroy. He wished to restore to the service the decency and awe which had been eroded by Puritanism and by sheer indifference. It was, he said, accounted superstitious for 'any man to come with more reverence into a church than a tinker and his bitch into an alehouse'.[10] He therefore wished to restore the visual richness of the church interior (or, at least, save the fabric from decrepitude) and the central place of communion in the service. Under Elizabeth the main stress had been on the sermon. Communion was usually celebrated around a table in the midst of the congregation, who received it seated. Laud ordered that the communion table should be placed altarwise at the east end of the church and railed off from the people, who were to receive communion kneeling. He thus tried to restore an element of mystery to the communion, which implied an elevated spiritual status for the priest who consecrated the bread and wine. In other ways, too, Laud wished to restore some of the authority over the laity which the clergy had lost since the Reformation and to revive the church courts as effective instruments of moral discipline. Finally, he placed great emphasis on hierarchy and authority within the Church and on the special role of bishops. To Puritans, bishops were a human invention, flawed like any other. To Laud, episcopal government was of divine institution, so without bishops there could be no true church.

Laud's programme was not original: other churchmen had argued that the Reformation had thrown out the good with the bad. Laud differed from his predecessors in having the determination and the power to impose his views, thanks to the support of Charles I. He thus split a broadly homogeneous Protestant Church into a Laudian minority, well established in positions of power, and a resentful Puritan majority. His assault on prevailing Puritan habits was so wide-ranging as to be obvious to all. Those who knew nothing of predestination would notice the moving and railing off of communion tables. Even the most indifferent might resent being asked to pay for repairs and embellishments, while the Laudians' heightened concern for the Church's property rights led to many clashes with lay people.[11] Inevitably, Laud's conduct led to accusations that he was bringing in Popery. The points on which he disagreed with the Catholics were far less obvious than those on which he agreed: even the pope was confused and offered to make him a cardinal. As Lord Falkland put it: 'Some have evidently laboured to bring in an English, though not a Roman, popery; I mean, not only the outside and dress of it but equally absolute, a blind dependence of the people upon the clergy'. Others saw Laudianism as just one step from Catholicism: 'There must be a conjunction between Papists and Protestants in doctrine, discipline and ceremonies; only it must not yet be called Popery'.[12]

The resentment which Laud's conduct aroused at all levels of society could find little expression before 1640. The press was muzzled and those who dared to criticise Laud's regime were severely punished (4). His opponents could voice their grievances only when Parliament was recalled in 1640. Ironically, it was Laud who helped to bring that about: his attempts to impose an English prayer book on Scotland provoked a revolt which eventually forced Charles to summon Parliament. Laud was impeached and later tried and executed (*10, 11*), while even before the end of 1640 there were petitions for the abolition of bishops (6). The future of the Church was now in Parliament's hands.

3. THE RISE OF THE SECTS

The men of the Long Parliament agreed that Laud's regime had been intolerable but could not agree on what to put in its place. Many would have liked to return to the moderate Puritanism of Elizabeth's reign, perhaps with the bishops sharing their power with the lower clergy. Unfortunately the existing bishops showed no inclination to share their power with anyone and Charles soon declared against any major changes in the Church.[13] The difficulty of reforming the existing system led some to argue that the only way to purge the Church of Laud's innovations was to abolish episcopacy 'root and branch'. The 'root and branch men' had no coherent or agreed scheme for a new form of church government, but that did not seem important. English Protestantism had long contained strong millenarian elements. The prophecies of Daniel and Revelation were believed to hold the key to the history of the world. The chronology of Foxe's *Book of Martyrs* was based on those prophecies and Napier used his logarithms to calculate the number of the Beast. Most saw in the Thirty Years' War the final struggle between the forces of Christ and of Antichrist which would end only with the end of the world. Opinions differed as to when the end would come, but few doubted that it was imminent.

Laud's fall and the other dramatic events of 1640–2 had an obvious significance to men steeped in apocalyptic prophecies. Antichrist was being overthrown, ushering in the rule of the saints, who would prepare for Christ's second coming and the Day of Judgment. God's purpose, long foretold, was now being worked out. Moreover, many believed that God not only had an overall plan for world history, not only predetermined who should be saved or damned, but also intervened constantly in daily life. A large literature of 'providences' showed 'the admirable judgements of God upon the transgressors of his commandments'.[14] To those who believed that God directed earthly affairs, guiding the virtuous and chastising the wicked, there seemed little need to worry about the precise form of church polity which would replace episcopacy: God would provide. Preachers to the Long Parliament made few specific proposals, confining themselves to general exhortations to do God's work.[15]

While the Westminster Assembly of Divines deliberated at length the question of church reform, others revelled in the freedom created by the collapse of Laud's regime. The Puritans had a tradition of religious exercises and prayer meetings outside the framework of parish worship. The absence of effective ecclesiastical authority and the apocalyptic hopes engendered by Laud's fall gave a double stimulus to such meetings – gatherings of like-minded believers who met to pray, discuss and seek God in their own way. Some were led by ordained ministers, others by laymen (or even women). Some were based on a parish church, others cut across parish boundaries. Some continued the orthodox Calvinism of the Elizabethan Church, others did not (practising adult baptism, for example). Such gatherings were very fluid, influenced greatly by the personality of their leaders. They were characterised more by spiritual commitment and intensity than by adherence to any doctrine or form of service. These 'gathered churches' saw themselves as 'the elect', 'visible saints' marked out by their zeal and spiritual purity from the unregenerate masses around them. They thus tended more and more to separate from parish congregations in which elect and reprobate were mixed indiscriminately: 'He that will not separate from the world and false-worship is a separate from Christ'.[16]

Independency (or Congregationalism) grew out of habits which began long before 1640. It reflected a hunger for religious discussion and experience, typified by an insatiable appetite for long sermons. It reflected, too, English Puritans' limited interest in forms of church government. To Cromwell the form of government, whether in church or state, was 'but a moral thing . . . as St Paul says "dross and dung in comparison with Christ"'. Nor were Independents over-concerned with details of theology: 'Love to all saints shows union with Christ'.[17] They became less flexible in the 1650s, faced with sects which seemed either dangerously heterodox or a threat to the stability of state and society. By the 1650s, too, their hopes that God would establish the rule of the saints and restore the 'old glorious beautiful face of Christianity' had been dashed.[18] In the 1640s, however, freedom had not yet hardened into sectarianism and the gathered churches offered Puritans spiritual exhilaration after the restrictions of the Laudian Church.

The growth of separatism posed a challenge to whatever national church the Westminster Assembly might devise. The gathered churches, being for the elect few, were incompatible with any parish-based system which, by definition, included sinners as well as saints. The inevitable hostility of the gathered churches was not the Assembly's only problem. In September 1643, with the war against the king going badly, Parliament signed the Solemn League and Covenant with the Scots (8). This brought much-needed military aid, but at a price. The Scots clergy (unlike the English) wielded great political power and had dogmatic views about church government. They expected Parliament to reconstruct the English Church on strict presbyterian lines. The Scots church was governed by a hierarchy of committees – presbyteries (representing groups of parishes), regional synods and a national General Assembly. This hierarchical system made possible a large measure of centralisation and the General Assembly also exercised great influence in secular politics. Such a system was anathema to most English Puritans. On one hand, it would destroy the traditional freedom of preachers and congregations to adapt the service to suit their own tastes, a freedom already threatened by Laud. On the other, it would give the clergy far greater power than had been normal in England. At every level, laymen were deeply involved in the English Church, from Parliament (which legislated for it) to the parishes where, more often than not, a layman nominated the parson or received at least part of the tithes. Here again the Scots' demands threatened, in a different way, a state of affairs already threatened by Laud.

Faced by the demand to reform the English Church on Scottish lines, Parliament took refuge in ambiguity, agreeing to reform the English Church 'according to the Word of God and the example of the best reformed churches'.[19] The Scots, of course, regarded their own as one of 'the best reformed churches' and pressed, in vain, for thoroughgoing changes. The Prayer Book was replaced by the Scottish 'Directory' and bishops were abolished, but that was the least Parliament could do to honour its promises. The settlement which emerged in 1648 was denounced by the Scots as a 'lame Erastian presbytery'. It allowed greater autonomy to individual congregations than existed in Scotland and the system was firmly under the control of lay 'elders' nominated by Parliament. By the time the scheme had been finalised, the matter had become largely academic. The New Model Army was about to seize the political initiative and would take no steps to implement the new system, which thus existed only on paper except in London and parts of Lancashire.[20]

The English Presbyterians of the 1640s rejected the centralisation and rigour of the Scots system but offered little in its place except confusion and contradiction. Most would have been content with a 'limited episcopacy' and some modifications to the

Prayer Book – a return to the normal practice of Elizabeth's reign. The intransigence of Charles I on one hand and the Scots on the other made such a settlement (traditional in practice, if not in form) impossible, so Parliament concocted a non-episcopal scheme designed to achieve the same ends. This sought to combine a limited congregational autonomy with a measure of authority and discipline. Conservative Puritans were alarmed at the multiplication of gathered churches. Propagandists like Thomas Edwards painted them in lurid and distorted colours and depicted them as a cancer eating away traditional moral and spiritual values. Discipline was needed to suppress practices which threatened the religious and social values for which moderate Puritans had always stood. The presbyterian ideal was of a parish in which the minister and leading laymen maintained discipline over the parishioners, while enjoying a limited autonomy in the way they conducted the parish's affairs.

The Presbyterian ideal differed from the Independent ideal in several ways. First, while the Presbyterians were not rigid about doctrine, they were less flexible than the Independents. Secondly, a Presbyterian congregation would include all the people of the parish, not 'visible saints' drawn from several parishes. Thirdly, while Independents practised voluntary self-discipline, each submitting to the censure of his fellows, Presbyterian discipline depended on the authority vested in minister and elders. It was the egalitarianism of the gathered churches which made them seem dangerous: 'If we make a parity in the church we must come to a parity in the commonwealth'.[21] Presbyterianism sought to re-establish the authority in ecclesiastical affairs on which social and political subordination depended and which the bishops had shown themselves unfit to exercise. By associating laymen with the minister, it guarded against the abuse of clerical power. The problem was that such a system depended on active lay support and on the backing of the state. Time was to show the impossibility of recruiting enough lay elders, while the regimes of 1649–60 had little sympathy for Presbyterianism. Without effective government support Presbyterianism was inoperable: one could not have a system based on parish discipline if people could opt out.[22]

When Laud fell, his system of censorship fell with him. The 1640s saw an explosion of publications, many of them illustrated. Opponents of episcopacy denounced Laud's regime and alleged that the bishops were Papists (6, 7, 9). After the Solemn League and Covenant it was clear that episcopacy was doomed and attention switched to what should replace it. Presbyterians exaggerated the number and strangeness of the sects, with allegations of sexual licence and depravity (14, 16). They depicted the Independents as both malicious and foolish (17). The Independents likened Presbyterian persecution to that of the bishops or the Papists: 'New presbyter is but old priest writ large' (20). Accusations of Popery flew in all directions. Not only were bishops reviled as Popish, but Presbyterians claimed that the gathered churches were organised by Jesuits who sought to destroy Protestantism by dividing it from within. A similar claim appeared in an Episcopalian print of 1645 (15). Amid such invective, much of it far-fetched, pleas for Protestants to unite against the common enemy, Popery, were few and little heeded (18).

As the 1640s wore on, hopes of godly regeneration were replaced by bewilderment and pessimism. God should have provided guidance, but He had not. One sign of pessimism was an obsession with the Devil and his works, seen in a sharp, if localised, revival of witchcraft prosecutions (*19*). Meanwhile, the Independents' claim that free discussion would lead to truth and consensus was contradicted by the appearance of sects too extreme for most Independents to stomach. The Ranters took predestination to its logical conclusion, arguing that the elect had no need of the Bible, worship or church organisation. They claimed that the elect were incapable of sin – indeed, to sin without guilt was a sign that one was chosen. 'Sin hath its conception only in the imagination . . . No matter what Scripture, saints or churches say, if that within thee do not condemn thee thou shalt not be condemned.'[23] Stories of orgies, violence and drunken parodies of communion were eagerly seized on by publishers, ever on the lookout for the lewd and sensational (*21, 22*).

The Ranters' heyday was short, but the opprobrium they attracted was soon transferred to the Quakers. They too relied on inward inspiration ('the inner light') rather than the Bible. Their meetings, like those of the Ranters, could be highly emotional, with shakings and convulsions as the spirit moved them. While avoiding the Ranters' sexual licence, the Quakers showed a penchant for outrageous conduct (like going naked 'for a sign'). Their refusal to doff their hats to magistrates, their use of the familiar 'thou' and their habit of bawling out clergymen in their churches challenged the dominant figures of authority in rural society, the squire and the parson. As the Quakers, like the Ranters, repudiated conventional 'Bible-Christianity' and threatened the social order, they were repressed with great severity. If they survived in numbers where the Ranters did not, this owed much to the organising skills of George Fox. He gave the Quakers a discipline and sense of identity which might seem incompatible with their stress on inner inspiration, but which ensured their survival. Under Fox's influence they also abandoned their more sensational conduct for a stubborn, conscientious quietism. At first, however, it was this sensationalism which appealed to print-makers (*23, 24*). Like other sects, the Quakers were also accused of being a creation of the Jesuits, designed to divide and discredit Protestantism.[24]

By the early 1650s English Protestantism had fragmented to an extent which would have seemed inconceivable fifteen years before. Sectarian divisions hardened with controversy and established congregations sought to retain their members. This hardening was especially apparent in relation to the Baptists and Quakers. Among more moderate Puritans there remained vestiges of the consensus and mutual tolerance of Elizabeth's day. This doubtless owed something to government policy in the 1650s. Cromwell saw himself as God's chosen instrument, but was reluctant to presume upon God's favour to the extent of establishing a 'rule of the saints'. He tried it once and it was a fiasco. His instinct was to preserve existing institutions and to stress the common ground shared by Protestants rather than the differences between them. He looked more indulgently than most on the more eccentric sects: 'Fear lest error should step in is like the man who would keep all the wine out of the country lest men should be drunk.'[25] He resisted Presbyterian demands for further statutory measures against religious minorities. In practice, Catholics, Anglicans, Quakers, even Jews enjoyed toleration, provided they posed no threat to the state.

If Cromwell refused to establish an official form of worship to which all should conform, he also refused to abolish the parish system and the tithes which supported it. He thus preserved the framework of a national church without laying down what it should teach or how it should be run and without providing any means of forcing people to attend its services. The choice of ministers, as in the 1640s and before, was left mainly to the dominant men of the localities, subject only to the ministers' reaching certain moral and educational standards. If there was any policy behind this, it was perhaps a hope that, given time, a new Puritan consensus might emerge, leaving the extremists isolated. Such hopes were not wholly unrealistic. Presbyterians and Independents were not entirely dogmatic about doctrine and church government. Many had been ordained before 1640 and could draw on a common Puritan tradition and a common dislike of Quakerism and Popery. Many who would have preferred moderate episcopacy were ready to accept Cromwell's system as the best they could reasonably expect. There was often close co-operation at a local level, as in Baxter's Worcestershire Association. Discussions about reunion at a national level broke down only in 1659. Even so, the changes and animosities of two decades could not easily be smoothed away and the political failure of Cromwell's regime removed the last chance to establish a Puritan national church. When the Church of England was restored in 1662, it was to be on very different lines.[26]

4. THE RESTORATION SETTLEMENT

Cromwell had reimposed censorship and there are virtually no prints critical of his religious policy. At the Restoration the licensing system was reintroduced. For twenty years almost no prints appeared on religious topics, for these were usually also politically sensitive. There is no doubt that the Restoration was popular. Whatever Charles I's faults, his death provided the royal cause with a martyr, a fact skilfully exploited by print-makers (25). Cromwell's regime had won acquiescence rather than support. It depended too blatantly on the army, unpopular in itself and the cause of the high level of taxation. Cromwell's obsession with security and the zeal of some officials led to a sporadic repression of centres of local conviviality, much resented by those who used them. A Sussex peasant, found in the alehouse on Sunday morning, said he would go to church only if beer were provided.[27] The army leaders, conscious of their unpopularity, had been unwilling to trust themselves to an unfettered electorate.[28] In the end, they united against them the Royalists and many moderate Parliamentarians. In religious terms, a mixture of Anglicans and Presbyterians brought about the Restoration.

Religion had been one – but only one – of the factors dividing Royalist and

Parliamentarian in 1642. Although many Royalists hated Laudianism, the Laudians could hardly support Parliament. In 1642 only a small minority of laymen adhered to Laud's style of Anglicanism, with its stress on ritual and authority. By 1660 their number had grown. This owed something to Laudian clergymen who, expelled from their parishes, served as chaplains to noble or gentry families. Secondly, the generation educated in Laudian Oxford and Cambridge had now grown up. A third reason was more social and political than ecclesiastical. All attempts to devise an effective system of church government in place of episcopacy had failed. England had teetered on the verge of anarchy, the world had (nearly) been turned upside down. There had been challenges to every aspect of conventional morality and to the existing social and political order. To nobles and gentlemen the lesson seemed clear: only episcopacy could ensure that subordination in the church which was vital for the maintenance of subordination in society.

This became clear in the strongly Royalist 'Cavalier House of Commons' elected in 1661. Charles II hoped, for reasons of political prudence, to modify the Church's liturgy and government so as to make them more acceptable to Presbyterians. The Commons would have none of it. The Prayer Book of 1662 was similar to that of 1559 and it was to be interpreted in a Laudian sense. One reason for this liturgical conservatism was a belief that 'a constant complete liturgy mightily conduceth to the edification and salvation as well as unanimity and peace of the meaner sort of people'.[29] Similarly, the bishops were not to share their authority with the lower clergy (although Parliament was also careful to limit the bishops' temporal power). Thus the opportunity to make the Church more comprehensive, to rebuild the loose consensus of Elizabeth's reign, was deliberately neglected. Indeed, after the fragmentation of 1640–60 such a consensus was probably unattainable. Any chance of reconciliation was further reduced by the Commons' rejection of Charles's attempts to grant toleration to those – Independents, Baptists, Quakers – who wanted no part in any national church. Instead Parliament passed a series of acts forbidding these 'Dissenters' (including the Presbyterians) to worship publicly and excluding them from municipal and other public offices.[30]

After 1660 the Church of England could no longer claim to include all English Protestants or even all those who believed in a national church. Internally, too, it was divided. On one hand, the High Churchmen were determined to adhere to Laudian ritual and the Laudian vision of the Church as the sole legitimate source of spiritual and moral authority. On the other hand, there were the Low Churchmen and Latitudinarians. The former were traditional Puritans, who remained within the Church but conformed somewhat selectively to its practices. Ralph Josselin, rector of Earl's Colne, almost never wore a surplice between 1660 and his death in 1683. Thomas Papillon, a layman of Huguenot descent, denounced 'all those that cry up the Church of England in opposition to the churches of Christ in foreign parts, that press the forms and ceremonies more than the doctrines of the Church, which are sound and scriptural'. Papillon had no objection to episcopacy, only to the conduct of the present bishops: 'When such are in place as promote true religion and piety, the Church will flourish and the clergy will be reverenced'.[31]

Papillon's outlook was similar to that of most Elizabethan Puritans. The Latitudinarians, too, shared some of these sentiments. Like Low Churchmen, they had little emotional attachment to the Church's rituals and felt a considerable affinity with both Dissenters, who rejected those rituals, and continental Calvinist churches which, to High Churchmen, were not true churches because they lacked bishops. Low Churchmen continued the Puritan emphasis on the Bible, preaching and enthusiasm. Latitudinarians, however, had no time for enthusiasm. They approached the Bible with neither wholehearted literalism nor inner inspiration, but with cool reason. Conscious that scientific discoveries cast doubt on some parts of the Bible and weary of the controversies of the Interregnum, they concentrated on the practical, moral aspects of Christianity. Where Puritans traditionally stressed God's vengeful and unpredictable intervention in human affairs, Latitudinarians saw His conduct as benevolent and rational. Where Puritans stressed the difficulty of measuring up to God's standards in a sinful world, Latitudinarians argued that it was easy to meet God's requirements. Indeed, it was not only easy but agreeable and profitable, for upright conduct brought tangible benefits. For Puritans life was a trial in which one might be tortured by doubts about one's salvation and for which the rewards could come only in the after-life. For Latitudinarians the world was a pleasant place, which could be enjoyed with profit provided one observed a few simple rules. Their outlook was summed up by the text for Tillotson's most popular sermon: 'For His commandments are not grievous'. Latitudinarian moral teaching was conventional, if tepid by Puritan standards. The way in which it was taught was quite new. By taking the fire and anguish out of religion, the Latitudinarians did much to shape the character of the eighteenth-century Church.[32]

5. 'POPERY AND ARBITRARY GOVERNMENT'

The reappearance of religious themes in the prints came with the biggest political crisis of Charles II's reign. His brother and heir apparent, James, Duke of York, became a Catholic which raised the prospect of the first Catholic monarch since Mary. The revelation of an alleged 'Popish Plot' to murder Charles made that prospect immediate, rather than a distant possibility, and led to a series of attempts to exclude James from the succession. As both Lords and king were hostile to Exclusion, the Exclusionists (or Whigs) sought to arouse popular support and to use it to intimidate their opponents (the Tories). This appeal to public opinion was made easier by the lapsing of licensing in 1679. Despite sporadic harassment by the courts, pamphlets and prints poured from the presses. The Whigs exploited the Plot to the full, to show the horrors which England had providentially avoided (27). They claimed that even worse horrors would ensue if James became king. He would advance his religion by violence, ignore the laws and raise an army that would make him as absolute as Louis XIV (30). The message of the prints was repeated in huge pageants in which the pope was burned in effigy (29). As time went on, the Whigs attacked not only James and the Catholics but also the Tories, whose opposition to Exclusion became more stubborn and effective. Especial venom was directed against the forthright Tory journalist, Roger L'Estrange (29–31). The Tories, frightened by the Whigs' demagogy, claimed that their true aim was to start another civil war, to overthrow Church and crown and to establish another tyranny like Cromwell's. Such allegations were given credence by the Whigs' sympathy for Dissenters and their attacks on the conduct of bishops and other High Churchmen. Thus while the Whigs identified the Tories with Popery and absolutism, the Tories identified the Whigs with Dissent and republicanism and revived the old accusation that Dissent had been fomented by Papists (28, 32, 33).[33]

In the end the Whigs' propaganda campaign failed. Tory support and Whig unwillingness to resort to force enabled Charles to emerge triumphant. Helped by the Tories, he harassed the Whigs and persecuted the Dissenters. In 1685 James II became king. He had often assured the Tories that he would uphold the Church's interests, but he soon made it clear that in return he expected Anglicans to acquiesce in measures that would give Catholics freedom of worship and full civil and political rights. This most Anglicans would not do. They thought it suicidal to remove the laws excluding Catholics from offices, for once in power they might use their authority to persecute Protestants. Since the Anglicans would not co-operate, James appealed to the Dissenters, offering a general toleration in return for their help in repealing the laws against Catholic and Dissenting worship, together with the Test Acts, which kept Catholics out of offices and out of Parliament. This completed the alienation of the Anglicans but won over few Dissenters. Most Dissenters hated Popery and were as reluctant as Anglicans to put Catholics in a position to harm them. Moreover, James's heir presumptive (his daughter Mary), and her husband, William, assured the Dissenters of their commitment to toleration, while urging them to preserve the Test Acts. Most Dissenters resisted James's advances and heeded those of the bishops, who now claimed that persecution had been a great mistake. Dissenters' suspicion of James increased when his queen gave birth to a son, who would be raised as a Catholic and take precedence over Mary in the succession. As the queen had not been pregnant for some years, many Protestants regarded the pregnancy as a Popish trick and the child as spurious (34). Meanwhile, James goaded the bishops into open defiance. He required them to order their clergy to read his Declaration of Indulgence to their parishioners and thus endorse publicly James's destruction of the Church's power to compel everyone to attend its services. Seven bishops petitioned James to change his mind. They were prosecuted for seditious libel and acquitted amid popular rejoicing. The appearance of a print of the bishops (35) showed that censorship was breaking down, thanks mainly to pamphlets imported from Holland. These pamphlets helped prepare the way for William of Orange's invasion, which led James to flee to France. Early in 1689 Parliament recognized William and Mary as joint monarchs. England had been saved from 'French tyranny and Popish oppression' (36).

6. 'THE CHURCH IN DANGER'

With the Glorious Revolution the immediate danger from Popery and absolutism receded. The threat lingered so long as the exiled Stuarts could attract help from abroad and so long as British Jacobites would conspire or rebel on their behalf. Even so, Jacobitism was only an occasional theme in the prints, appearing mainly at times of plot or invasion. The major religious themes under William III and Anne stemmed from divisions within the Church and from the religious legislation of 1689.

The Revolution embarrassed High Churchmen for reasons both political and religious. Under Charles II they had exalted the crown's authority, for only a strong monarchy seemed capable of holding down the radical forces in society and preventing another civil war. They insisted that the Bible forbade subjects to resist their lawful ruler: if he behaved unjustly, they must submit. Faced with James's ill-treatment of the Church, however, the Seven Bishops had shown that they were prepared to defy their king. The Tories' attitude to William's invasion had been ambivalent. Most accepted his assurances that he came, not to seize the crown, but to call a free parliament. Few Tories opposed William: some even rose against James, yet most were conscious that such conduct ran counter to Tory principles: 'How these risings . . . can be justified I see not; but yet it is very apparent, had not the Prince come and these persons thus appeared, our religion had been rooted out.'[34] James's departure left High Churchmen with mixed feelings. Few wanted him back, but most saw William as a usurper and were reluctant to recognise him as 'rightful and lawful' king, as opposed to king *de facto*. A large minority of the clergy (including five of the Seven Bishops) refused to swear allegiance to William. These 'non-jurors' lost their benefices and remained a living reproach to less rigorous High Churchmen who took the oath.

The Revolution also left High Churchmen embarrassed in ecclesiastical matters. In countering James's appeals to the Dissenters, they had made offers from which they could not honourably retreat. They were prepared, in 1689, to modify the Church's liturgy and practice in order to comprehend moderate Dissenters within the Church, while allowing toleration to those who wished to remain outside. This scheme was wrecked by William's tactlessness. He showed High Churchmen little consideration and his demands for the removal of Dissenters' political disabilities effectively killed the comprehension bill. Only the toleration bill became law. It allowed Dissenters freedom of worship under certain conditions. Their ministers had to subscribe those of the Thirty-Nine Articles which dealt with doctrine: in practice, this excluded only those who denied the Trinity. Meeting houses had to be licensed and the doors kept open during meetings (so that sedition could not be plotted under pretence of religion) (37). The existing laws remained in force and all who did not meet these conditions were subject to them. No relief was granted to Catholics, nor were the political disabilities on Dissenters removed. To qualify for office Dissenters had to renounce the Covenant and take communion according to the Anglican rite.[35]

The Toleration Act was a severe psychological blow to High Churchmen. No longer could the Church claim even a theoretical monopoly of religious life. The Act did not lead to a large increase in the number of Dissenters, but Church attendance fell considerably as the apathetic or uninterested stayed away. Resentment at the weakening of the Church's authority was increased by what High Churchmen saw as a systematic campaign against it. William appointed moderates or Low Churchmen to bishoprics. The laws against Dissenters' holding office were evaded by occasional conformity, whereby a Dissenter took Anglican communion once a year to qualify for office. The Toleration Act contained no prohibition of Dissenting schools, so that the Church's monopoly of education now survived only in the universities. The last vestige of clerical control over the press (the licensing of theological works by a senior ecclesiastic) disappeared when the last Licensing Act lapsed in 1695. A few works were published which challenged the need for revealed religion and even questioned the existence of God. The post-Revolution period was one of an unusually questioning spirit. Locke challenged the traditional Christian concepts of original sin and innate ideas and argued that one's values were the product of environment and education. Locke was no atheist, but his religion was shorn of all mysticism: in *The Reasonableness of Christianity* he claimed that Christian doctrine could be reduced to the single truth that Jesus was the Messiah. Such views were not confined to laymen. Samuel Clarke, despite having subscribed the Thirty-Nine Articles, denied the divinity of Christ (39). Benjamin Hoadly saw private judgment and personal sincerity as the sole determinants of religious truth, a view which rendered churches, with their doctrines, liturgies and institutions, irrelevant. It also removed any reason for persecution. For High Churchmen, who stressed the authority conferred by the Church's continuity with the pre-Reformation Church, such views were as hateful as Hoadly's lack of interest in the rituals which they found spiritually satisfying. Their complaints that Hoadly betrayed all that the Church stood for were given an added edge by the fact that Hoadly eagerly sought preferment within the Church whose needfulness he denied (41–3).

High Churchmen, then, believed that the Revolution had weakened the Church's moral influence so that atheism, deism and immorality could flourish. As William's bishops would not act resolutely, the High Churchmen turned to political action, through Parliament and Convocation. Throughout Anne's reign religion was a major political issue. The Whigs sought to preserve or extend the Toleration Act, by naturalising foreign Calvinists or allowing toleration to Dissenters in Ireland. The Tories wanted, at the least, to close the loopholes in the Act.

The disputes of High and Low Church, Whig and Tory were political as well as religious. The Tories retained their emotional veneration for monarchy. Anne, the last Protestant Stuart, was to them queen by divine hereditary right. Tory parsons again preached non-resistance. The snag, from the Tory point of view, was that Anne had no children. To keep out James's Catholic son, the Old Pretender, Parliament decreed that on Anne's death the crown should pass to the House of Hanover. High Churchmen did not want another Catholic, but their legitimist souls recoiled at the prospect of a foreigner with a remote hereditary claim. Some hoped that the Pretender might reconcile the conflict between legitimacy and Protestantism by turning Protestant, but he never did. The High Churchmen were therefore torn between emotional attachment to the Stuarts and a practical awareness that another Catholic would be intolerable. Their discomfiture allowed the Whigs to argue that the Tories were Jacobites and that the triumph of High Church principles would bring in Popery and absolutism (*40*). The Tories, meanwhile, revived the equation between Whiggery and Dissent and republicanism (*39, 41*), particularly denouncing clergymen who failed to defend their High Church viewpoint (*44*). Their arguments were given added plausibility by those Whigs who, goaded by Tory assertions of non-resistance, propounded radical political views and upheld the people's right to resist a tyrant.[36] These controversies reached a climax in the trial of Dr Sacheverell.

Henry Sacheverell was one of the most intemperate High Church parsons to emerge from Oxford. In a sermon before the Lord Mayor of London on 5 November 1709 he ranged widely, if incoherently, over the dangers facing the Church and asserted 'the utter illegality of resistance upon any pretence whatsoever'. On the anniversary of William's landing (which to many exemplified that resistance could be justified), this was a challenge which a Whig ministry could not ignore. Sacheverell was impeached and his trial called into question both the condition of the Church and what had happened at the Revolution. The sermon itself sold a hundred thousand copies and aroused huge public interest (*45, 47*). Most of the prints favoured Sacheverell and the London populace was clearly on his side. On 1 March a well-organized crowd sacked several Dissenting meeting houses and attacked the dwellings of Hoadly and other leading Whigs (*46*). The rioters were encouraged by sermons on such texts as 'Break their teeth, O God, in their mouths'. The riots did not affect the verdict: Sacheverell was found guilty, but given only a token sentence. They did illustrate the immense popular support which now existed for High Church views, which doubtless owed much to the many parsons who had been educated at Oxford, since the Restoration the bastion of High Churchmanship. As one Low Church bishop wrote: 'Before those civil wars none ran into these notions but some of the warmer and ambitious clergy; whereas now the common people and the very women had their heads full of them'.[37]

The Sacheverell trial inaugurated a brief period in which Tories and High Churchmen carried all before them. They won crushing election victories in 1710 and 1713, confirming that they had the support of a majority of the largest and freest electorate that England was to see before 1832, but their hour of triumph was brief. With George I's accession the Whigs gained a monopoly of power. They manipulated the electoral system so that the Tories became a permanent, isolated minority in the Commons. All senior ecclesiastical posts went to Whigs. Convocation was suppressed. The Whigs had learned from the Sacheverell trial, however, that Dissenters were unpopular. Ministers like Walpole did little for them, for it was politically unwise to antagonise the Churchmen. Religion, therefore, played only an intermittent part in politics for the rest of the century, a fact reflected by the spasmodic appearance of religious subjects in the prints. The style of prints changed too. The intricate and often heavily allegorical concoctions of the seventeenth century became unfashionable. Improved standards of draughtsmanship and engraving meant the end of the crude little woodcuts which had flourished during the Interregnum. If many prints were still complex and even cluttered, most were simpler in composition without being crude in execution. From the mid-century, English cartoonists began to adopt the Italian practice of caricature, distorting and exaggerating the features of those portrayed, thus adding an extra dimension of cruelty and mockery to personal attacks which were already often vicious and unfair. With the end of censorship and the vast increase in the number of prints produced, popular prints offer a detailed commentary on high politics. On religious subjects that commentary was much less full and even less reliable.

II.
The Eighteenth Century
1714–c.1780

1. THE CHURCH OF ENGLAND

The High Church agitations of Anne's reign were the last spasm of the religious controversies and enthusiasms of the seventeenth century. The outlook of the eighteenth was cooler, more cynical and more secular. Walpole and the Pelhams developed a system of political management less dependent on ideological or moral principles than any before or since. A similar cynicism was apparent with regard to the clergy. Church preferments were places, like any others, to be disposed of for political advantage. Clergymen were depicted as rogues, interested only in money (*48*). Yet it would be wrong to see this as an irreligious age. That arch electoral organiser, the Duke of Newcastle, worried greatly about spiritual matters and took great care preparing for communion.[38] The leaders of society still believed in God and attended church, albeit less assiduously than in the past, but the emotional intensity and excitement of religion had declined. The Latitudinarian approach had triumphed, with its reliance on reason and its undemanding, prudential moral teaching. The benefit which Hogarth's industrious apprentice derived from attending church was not spiritual fulfilment but the company of his master's daughter (*51*). (He later married her and took over the business.) By taking the pain and anxiety out of religion, the Latitudinarians all too often made it deadly dull: the sleeping congregation was a favourite topic for satirists (*49, 50*). Addison, however, saw the Sunday service as the high point of a village's week and

the best method that could have been thought of for the polishing and civilizing of mankind. It is certain the country people would soon degenerate into a kind of savages and barbarians, were there not such frequent returns of a stated time in which the whole village meet together with their best faces and in their cleanliest habits to converse with one another upon different subjects, hear their duties explained to them and join together in adoration of the Supreme Being.[39]

In a country church one saw the community on its knees, with all its social gradations: the squire and wealthier farmers in their pews, the labourers on their benches, worshipping together. Yet the emphasis is on social and moral control, rather than the sharing of eternal spiritual truths: religion, to Addison, is useful rather than inspiring.

The corollary of the Latitudinarians' prudential moral teaching was a lack of interest in dogma:

For modes of faith let graceless zealots fight:
He can't be wrong whose life is in the right.

The volume and intensity of theological controversy diminished. The few Anglican clergymen who held heterodox views not only remained unmolested but prospered.

Hoadly ended up bishop of Winchester and Clarke, too, came close to a bishopric. Parliament, however, rejected a petition to remove the need for ordinands to subscribe the Thirty-Nine Articles (*117*).

The Hoadlys and Clarkes were not typical of eighteenth-century Anglican clergymen, whose fault was mediocrity rather than heterodoxy. Many of the Church's problems stemmed from the inequitable distribution of resources, compounded by the laity's ambivalent attitude towards church preferments. Much of the Church's vast wealth was concentrated in the hands of bishops and cathedral dignitaries. In many parishes part or all of the tithes were received by a layman who paid only a pittance to the parson. If the tithes went to a clergyman, he might not minister to the parish himself: indeed, the more lucrative the parish, the more likely it was that the incumbent would be an absentee who would pay a curate to discharge his priestly duties. Despite certain statutory limitations, pluralism (whereby one man held several benefices) was rife and with pluralism went non-residence. In 1809, 7,358 out of 11,194 parishes had no resident incumbent. Many of these were served by curates but in 1812 over a thousand were not, which meant that they were either looked after by a neighbouring parson or received no pastoral care at all.[40]

Pluralism and non-residence dated back to before the Reformation and had two main causes. The first was the use of church places as political rewards or to provide for the aristocracy's younger sons. The choicest places were bishoprics and those in cathedral chapters: 'The life of a prebendary is a pretty easy way of dawdling away one's time: praying, walking, visiting: and as little study as the heart could wish'.[41] Bishops and cathedral dignitaries could usually hold places in plurality but so could others, like the chaplains of peers. Thus one reason for pluralism was the greed and ambition of the well-connected (*54*). The other was the poverty or smallness of many parishes which made pluralism virtually an economic necessity. The lumping together of two adjacent poor parishes was very different from a dean accumulating rich and scattered livings, yet the two were often confused. Laymen were also perhaps too ready to condemn pluralism and non-residence without considering how far they were responsible for them. Some laymen received the tithes that should have gone to the parson: almost half of all tithes were impropriated in this way. Rich and influential laymen sought preferments for their kinsmen and clients, irrespective of their abilities, while others, slightly less rich and influential, possessed (or claimed) the right to choose the parson of their village and used it to provide for a member of the family.[42]

As the landed elite creamed off many of the best benefices, the work of ministering to the people was left mainly to curates. As the supply of would-be curates exceeded the demand, many were miserably paid and enjoyed no security of tenure. A favourite theme of satirists was the contrast between the affluent pluralist and the poor curate who did his work for him (*53–5*). There was a great social gulf between the wealthy rector, mixing with the gentry, and the poor curate, no better off than the small farmers and labourers among whom he lived. Another common object of satire was the way in which preferments were distributed. Those of gentle birth had few problems, but others needed an influential patron (59). Usually, learning and pastoral skills counted for little: the B.A. degree included no theology. Kinship, clientage and political loyalty were more important considerations, but there could be others, like the need to provide for disbanded officers after the American war (58). Bribery was probably rare (57). At the top political considerations were paramount, although politicians distinguished between 'bishoprics of business for men of abilities and learning, and bishoprics of ease for men of family and fashion'.[43] For the real plums, like Canterbury, there was fierce competition as ambitious clerics vied for the attention of the king's ministers (56).

The vices of the eighteenth-century church were not new, but perhaps seemed more glaring than before because of the undemonstrative character of eighteenth-century spiritual life. The lay religious societies of the early part of the century combined personal piety and mutual edification with a strongly practical Christianity. This was an 'age of benevolence', ranging in scale from Parson Woodforde's careful disbursement of parochial charity to the great new London hospitals established between 1710 and 1750. Along with a concern for the lower orders' physical well-being went a concern for their morals, seen in societies for the reformation of manners and the provision of specifically Christian elementary education, co-ordinated through the S.P.C.K. Determined individual clergymen, like Griffith Jones of Llanddowror with his 'circulating schools', achieved remarkable results on a tiny budget.[44] Such solid but unspectacular achievements, however, were of little interest to satirists. When all allowances are made, moreover, there was much to satirise. In an age of political promotions, it was easy to argue that the clergy were more interested in good living than in matters spiritual (62). Some parsons and churchwardens showed the same casual attitude to the moneys they handled as those in secular employments (60) or the same fondness for the alehouse as their parishioners (63). The problem was, perhaps, not that the Church's standards were lower than those of lay society, but that they were no higher.

As the clergy failed to set a moral and spiritual example, respect for the clerical order was at a low ebb. It was just as well that the clergy no longer claimed the moral authority over laymen which High Churchmen had earlier claimed. Claims of autonomy or that episcopal authority was divinely ordained were largely abandoned (64). The church courts functioned within the limits allowed by the common law courts, which typified the subordinate position which the clergy became accustomed to accept. If they claimed authority by virtue of their spiritual status or tried to exploit their property rights to the full, they provoked shrill complaints of clerical ambition or rapacity. This was shown by the experience of Edmund Gibson, bishop of London. Gibson advised Walpole on church matters (he was known as 'Walpole's pope') and was unusual – and perhaps inconsistent – in being both a Whig and a High Churchman. He opposed the pressure of George II's queen for the promotion of Hoadly, Clarke and others whom he thought heterodox or Latitudinarian. This inflamed the more extreme Whigs, who seized on his having written a massive work on canon law and claimed that, like Laud, he wished to exalt the clergy above the laity. It was no coincidence that the period of Gibson's ascendency saw a string of bills in the Commons to define procedure in the church courts and to weaken the clergy's position in disputes over property (65–6).[45]

Such outbreaks of anticlericalism were exceptional, provoked by rare hints of clerical independence. Usually the clergy were more submissive, accepting without question Parliament's claim to legislate on all matters ecclesiastical. Parsons followed the wishes of their patrons, promotions were milked of every ounce of political advantage, bishops served as obedient lobby-fodder in the Lords. There were many competent and conscientious pastors and some bishops of administrative and intellectual distinction, but such were incidental, even fortuitous, by-products of a Church which was in many ways run by the laity for the laity. The faults of the eighteenth-century Church were above all those of the society within which it operated. There was some spectacular neglect, but much quiet achievement. If some church buildings were on the verge of collapse, there is solid evidence of extensive church building and rebuilding, even in the remote diocese of Carlisle.[46] Nor did all contemporaries find the Anglican clergy contemptible. In the words of John Wesley:

Ever since the Reformation, and particularly in the present century, the behaviour of the clergy is greatly altered for the better . . . They have not only more learning of the most valuable kind, but abundantly more religion. Insomuch that the English and Irish clergy are generally allowed to be not inferior to any in Europe, for piety as well as for knowledge.[47]

2. OLD DISSENT

After the Toleration Act Dissent might have been expected to flourish, but after a brief flurry all denominations suffered a severe decline, losing perhaps half their membership between 1700 and 1740. This was due in part to factors which also affected the Church – a slackening of enthusiasm and a growth of heterodoxy, especially among the Presbyterians who, after 1689, accepted sectarian status as there was clearly no place for them in the Church. As they no longer felt compelled to think in 'national' terms, the Presbyterian tradition of allowing ministers a certain autonomy become more pronounced. The Presbyterians were also influenced more than other Dissenters by the intellectual developments which had given rise to Latitudinarianism. They became the most rational of Dissenters. Sometimes their reason led them into heterodoxy, especially Unitarianism, but even those ministers whose theology remained conventional proved reluctant to censure their brethren. Like the Latitudinarians they concentrated on basic morality rather than abstruse questions of doctrine.

Such developments led to a rift between the Presbyterians and Independents (or Congregationalists). As the Presbyterians responded to the 'spirit of the age' and moved further from their Puritan roots, most Congregationalists moved the other way and clung more tightly to orthodox Calvinism. They became introverted and tried to preserve the doctrinal purity of existing adherents rather than seeking new converts. A fitful dialogue with the Presbyterians ended at the Salters' Hall debates in 1719. Faced with the problem of whether to approve a Presbyterian ordinand with doubts about the Trinity, most of the Congregationalists came down firmly against any hint of Unitarianism, while most Presbyterians were more tolerant (67). Thereafter, the two denominations developed in different ways. The Presbyterians became the least orthodox of Dissenters, but in the process lost most of their popular support. Their congregations came to be dominated by the clergy and a few wealthy, well-educated laymen who preferred the ministers' polished, intellectual preaching to the Congregationalists' cruder, more fundamental Protestantism. Many poorer, less educated Presbyterians defected to the Congregationalists or Baptists where they found preachers more to their liking. The Quakers, too, lost much of their dynamism (68). They became solid and respectable, dominated by a few wealthy families. Like the Church, the Dissenters showed little interest in expansion. Unlike the Church, they had few adherents among the landed elite who could use their social authority to bring the poor to church.[48] Neither Church nor Dissent had much to offer those largely untouched by conventional religion, especially in the expanding mining and manufacturing villages. The spiritual needs of these people were to be met by the Methodists.

3. METHODISM

The old Dissenters scarcely appear in popular prints of the eighteenth century. The Methodists, by contrast, were the subject of many. Usually they were treated with hostility, but there was no denying their impact. On one hand, they revived Puritan traditions of evangelism and enthusiasm, largely forgotten with the triumph of Latitudinarianism and apathy. On the other, they showed that the growth of industrial communities opened up a new field for missionary endeavour. They also developed a novel organisation to sustain the momentum of their evangelism.

Methodism was the creation of the brothers John and Charles Wesley. Both Anglican clergymen, they came of a family in which High Church and Puritan piety were oddly mingled. At Oxford they formed the 'Holy Club', a lay society typical of the period, concerned with mutual edification and practical piety. In 1738, after periods of doubt and despondency, both underwent a sudden conversion which dramatically changed their lives. Soon after, John accepted an invitation from the evangelist George Whitefield to preach to the colliers of Kingswood, near Bristol. Whitefield was more flamboyant and histrionic than the Wesleys, who had known him at Oxford. His preaching had had a great impact on the colliers: 'They were glad to hear of a Jesus who . . .came not to call the righteous but sinners to repentance. The first discovery of their being affected was to see the white gutters made by their tears which plentifully ran down their black cheeks.'[49] Whatever his initial reservations about preaching outside the church, John Wesley soon decided that preaching to the poor was to be his life's work: 'I bear the rich and love the poor, therefore I spend all my time with them'.[50] He sought to communicate the faith which he had found in his conversion. Faith, to him, was 'not barely a speculative rational thing, a cold lifeless assent, a train of ideas in the head; but also a disposition of the heart . . . It is a sure confidence which a man hath in God that, through the merits of Christ, *his* sins are forgiven and *he* reconciled to the favour of God.'[51]

Wesley thus rediscovered what most Anglicans and Presbyterians had forgotten, that 'Christianity is more the religion of the heart than the head'. The preaching he offered was 'the old sort that comes like a thunderclap upon the conscience'.[52] His appeal to the emotions excited his audiences to tears, convulsions and strange cries, but also bred a joy and confidence which found expression in Charles Wesley's hymns. Wesley was attacked for his 'enthusiasm', which for most educated people was a term of abuse (*69, 70*). His concentration on the poor and his claims that rich and poor were spiritually equal were denounced as subversive. 'It is monstrous to be told you have a heart so sinful as the common wretches that crawl upon the earth', squawked one aristocratic lady.[53] In many places clergy and gentlemen incited mobs to attack the Methodists, who suffered violence and looting, yet at the same time they were accused of being trouble-makers and even Papists.[54] Their meetings were said to be disorderly and to attract criminals and other undesirables, while the preachers were alleged to be interested only in making money out of the poor and gullible (*71, 72, 74*). Few prints gave any hint of what Methodism meant to its adherents (*73*).

In many ways Wesley's outlook had much in common with that of seventeenth-century Puritans. In spite of – perhaps because of – rationalist challenges to the authenticity of the Bible, Wesley reaffirmed that it was the sole source of authority in matters spiritual. He shared the Puritan sense of human depravity and believed in possession by the Devil and in witches – 'Giving up witchcraft is, in effect, giving up the Bible'. (The last conviction for witchcraft had occurred in 1712.) Like most Puritans, Wesley was more interested in the quality of a person's faith than in his precise theological views. He imposed no doctrinal test for membership of Methodist societies: one just had to want to be saved. The one great difference was that Wesley's theology was Arminian, not Calvinist. Depraved though men were, God would enable them to recognize His laws, if their eyes were opened by suitable preaching. In many ways, Arminianism was a more logical basis than Calvinism for an evangelical movement: if God had foreordained who was to be saved, what was the point of seeking converts? To Wesley, conversion was crucial. Without repentance and the faith born of conversion, one could not hope to merit God's grace.[55]

One problem facing any movement which relies on emotion and the experience of conversion is that its effects are likely to prove ephemeral. It was part of John Wesley's genius that he developed an organisation to sustain the initial impact of Methodism. Each congregation (or 'society') had no permanent preacher but was part of a 'circuit' with an itinerant preacher, who changed every year or two. 'Were I myself to preach one whole year in one place,' wrote Wesley, 'I should preach both myself and most of my congregation asleep.'[56] To maintain spiritual intensity and discipline, each society was divided into smaller 'bands'. These were used both to raise funds and for mutual exhortation and collective self-discipline. With their high level of spiritual rigour, they contained echoes of the gathered churches of the 1640s. At the other end of the scale was the problem of co-ordinating the various circuits, a problem overcome by strict centralisation. The societies were controlled by the officials of the circuit, the circuits were subordinated to the 'district', the districts' affairs were directed by the 'connection' and all were subject to Wesley himself or, after his death, to the Conference. It was a system at once expansive and intensive, allowing for both uniform planning at a national level and the detailed supervision of particular societies. It all bore the imprint of Wesley's personality: 'As long as I live, the people shall have no share in choosing either stewards or leaders . . . We are no republicans and never intend to be.'[57]

Despite creating this elaborate organisation, Wesley had no wish to break with the Church of which he was a priest. He saw Methodist societies as serving a purpose similar to that of the lay societies, complementing the work of the Church, not competing with it. He urged his followers to hold their meetings outside normal service hours. He retained a great fondness for the Church's liturgy (here again differing from earlier Puritans). He received communion regularly and expected his followers to do the same. Many Methodists found his attitude hard to understand. They did not share his High Church background and were repelled by the hostility of many parsons. They resented meeting at inconvenient times and pressed Wesley to go into open competition with the Church. Wesley remained adamant. However illogical it might seem to try to reconcile one system based on the parish with another based on itinerancy, he refused to break with the Church. Only in his last years were there hints that he might change his mind.

Methodism made its greatest impact in industrial areas – in the West, the West Midlands and the North – where the Church was usually weak. It made almost no impact on the agricultural South and East, not least because Wesley ignored the region, believing agricultural workers to be irremediably stupid. In many ways, Methodism reflected the contradictions of Wesley's own personality: the mixture of a Puritan style of evangelism with a High Church fondness for ritual; the contrast between Wesley's spiritual egalitarianism and, on one hand, his authoritarian direction of the Methodist movement, and, on the other, his conservatism in secular politics (74). It may or may not be true that the conversion of working people to Methodism, an essentially conservative creed, made them less susceptible to the revolutionary ideas which soon swept through Europe. It is certainly true that the Methodists rediscovered the evangelical energy and moral seriousness of Puritanism. Thanks to their example that energy and seriousness were transmitted to others: to the Evangelicals within the Church and to the revivalists of the New Dissent.

4. ANTI-CATHOLICISM IN THE EIGHTEENTH CENTURY

In the eighteenth century even more than the seventeenth, anti-Catholicism was primarily political. While 'Popery' was disliked as alien and superstitious (77), most anti-Catholic prints were inspired by political events and served a specific propagandist purpose. The Jacobite risings of 1715 and 1745 provoked several. The '15 was a godsend to the Whigs, still unpopular after the latter part of Anne's reign. The Tories had then exploited popular war-weariness and concern for the Church, against which the Whigs' only real electoral asset was fear of Jacobitism. When George I became king the Whigs smeared the Tories indiscriminately as Jacobites, a tactic which helped them to win the election of 1715. The Jacobite rising later in the year enabled them to consolidate their hold on power. The Septennial Act of 1716 removed the need to face the electorate before 1722, by which time they had gained control of enough of the smaller boroughs to give them an unassailable majority in the Commons. The Riot Act made it much easier to use the military against rioters. Such measures showed the Whigs' consciousness of their unpopularity. They were unpopular partly because there was much sympathy for the Jacobites and Tories prosecuted after the '15, partly because the new German king and his regime seemed sordid and corrupt. The Whigs sought to revive their sagging political credit by anti-Catholicism and continued to hold pope-burning processions, a practice they had revived when their fortunes were at their nadir under Anne (76).[58]

As the Whigs' hold on power became impregnable, they still occasionally used anti-Catholicism. Walpole saw the common fear of Jacobitism as a means of uniting the warring Whig factions and of preventing any group from allying with the Tories. In time, popular support for the Pretender diminished and Jacobitism came to appear less dangerous. The initial success of the '45 came as an unpleasant shock. A sudden flurry of prints stressed the Pretender's links with France and depicted the tyranny and persecution that would ensue if his invasion succeeded (78–80). The repression which followed Culloden broke the back of Jacobite support in Scotland, just as the '45 had shown its bankruptcy in England. After 1746 Jacobitism largely disappeared from the prints and for thirty years anti-Popery appeared mainly in propaganda against France (81).

The reappearance of anti-Catholicism in 1778–80 was dramatic and surprising. For a century and a half most of the animus against Popery had derived from its association with royal tyranny or alien invasion, but such a connection largely disappeared after 1746. The English Catholics were few and innocuous. Most lived in villages dominated by Catholic landowners or in remote upland hamlets where the established church was weak. In most towns Catholics were few. The great Irish immigration of the industrial revolution had scarcely begun in 1780. Even in London, where there was a large cosmopolitan Catholic population, there had been no serious anti-Catholic violence since 1688. Skirmishes between English and Irish probably owed more to nationality than to religion.

It was thus surprising that 1780 saw a massive outburst of anti-Catholic violence. Its immediate occasion was the Catholic Relief Act of 1778, which removed a few of the legal restrictions on Catholics. It passed Parliament easily, but aroused violent antagonism in Scotland (82), which led Parliament to decide that it should not apply there. This retreat encouraged the extra-parliamentary opposition to the Act in England, expressed mainly through Lord George Gordon's Protestant Association and supported (among others) by Wesley (87). The Association's propaganda harped on traditional themes, like the cruelty of Popish persecution and the links between Popery and tyranny (83–4). On 2 June 1780 Gordon presented to Parliament a petition with sixty thousand signatures against the Act. The crowd which accompanied him was so large and menacing that Parliament adjourned for a few days, but Gordon's supporters were not inclined to be patient. Two Catholic ambassadors' chapels were burned, which proved only the start of several days' rioting. In time, the crowds extended their targets from Catholic chapels and the houses of prominent Catholics to prisons (releasing the prisoners) (89) and the toll-houses on Blackfriars Bridge. By the 8th there were ten thousand troops in London and by the end of the riots 285 people had been killed by the military. It was easy to argue that plunder was the rioters' main motive (85, 87, 89) and there was much wanton destruction and looting. Mostly, however, the rioters showed discrimination and discipline, attacking the property of Catholics or known supporters of the Relief Act and taking care not to damage adjacent property. It is also remarkable that nobody was killed by the rioters.[59]

The Gordon Riots remain difficult to explain satisfactorily. They owed much to the personal charisma of Gordon and to the widespread misapprehension that the Act would remove *all* the disabilities on Catholics. There was no clear pattern of hostility to the Irish, nor did the rioters concentrate on parishes where Catholics were most numerous. In the later stages the targets became less obviously 'Catholic': there were even plans (as in 1710) to attack the Bank of England. The riots lasted so long because the City government was slow to call in troops, either because it hoped to embarrass the government or because it remembered the prosecution of those who used force against the Wilkites. Soldiers were used only when the riots seemed to be getting out of hand.[60]

To the Protestant Association the rioters were patriots trying to save Protestantism despite the government's neglect (86). It even claimed that the riots were secretly instigated by Papists (88). In general, however, the riots alienated respectable opinion, especially when they became more indiscriminate. Even Wilkes eventually acted vigorously against the rioters in his capacity as a J.P. The Protestant Association's support declined, the Relief Act remained in force. Gordon himself became a Jew and died insane (90). The anti-Popish fury of 1780 soon came to seem oddly archaic. The irreligion of the French Revolution made the churches – even the Catholic Church – seem necessary bastions of the existing social and political order. French émigré priests were generously received in England. When English Catholic seminaries moved from France to England there was hardly a murmur of protest. There was little complaint either about the Catholic Relief Act of 1791, which exempted Catholics from the penal laws, provided they took an oath of allegiance. They could now open chapels, under certain conditions, but still could not hold public offices or vote in elections.[61] At last the old hostility to Catholicism seemed to be dying away. When anti-Popery re-emerged as a major feature of politics, it had been transformed by the Union with Ireland.

5. THE JEWS

If the Catholic minority was small, the Jewish minority was minute: only about eight thousand in 1750. After the Jews' expulsion from England in 1290, only a few isolated individuals had been naturalised. Under Cromwell they were allowed to open a synagogue in London but their legal position remained obscure. Most early immigrants were Sephardic Jews, of Spanish or Portuguese descent. Most were prosperous and many adopted English styles of dress and manners. In the eighteenth century pogroms in Central and Eastern Europe led to many Ashkenazim coming to England. Unlike the Sephardim these did not become Anglicised and were debarred by their religion from taking apprenticeships or receiving parish charity. They found work where they could, as pedlars or hawkers or dealers in old clothes, which often led to trafficking in stolen goods, a tendency heightened by their being forced by poverty to settle in areas of London where criminal activity was rife.[62]

There were thus two Jewish communities. First, a few wealthy Sephardim, partly integrated into polite society. Samson Gideon, for example, was the foremost banker of his day, closely associated with the Pelhams. His children were baptised as Christians and his son became an Irish peer. Then there were the obviously foreign Ashkenazim, many of them forced by poverty and their alien status into occupations of dubious legality. In the prints, there was no clear distinction between the two. Jews were depicted as criminals (*90, 92*) and hypocrites (*91*). Normally the dishonest Jew, like the greedy parson or ranting Methodist, was merely a stock figure of ridicule. Only with the Jew Bill controversy of 1753 did the satire become more concentrated and extreme.

The Jewish Naturalisation Act was designed to make it easier for individual Jews to apply for naturalisation and so escape the disadvantages suffered by alien merchants. Passed with the Pelhams' blessing, after lobbying by the London Sephardim, it removed the need for Jews to take Anglican communion or the Test in order to qualify for naturalisation. It was a limited and permissive measure and passed with little opposition. The outcry which it caused was totally unexpected. Like Walpole, the Pelhams avoided contentious policies, so that disgruntled politicians found it hard to find issues on which to attack them. The Jew Bill seemed the chance they had waited for. Its opponents appealed to long-standing prejudices against immigrants and to City merchants, fearful of the Jews' legendary business acumen. They imparted a specious integrity to their opposition by invoking religion. As the opposition campaign mounted, it was widely believed that the Act naturalized all Jews, instead of allowing individuals to apply for naturalization, which might be refused. It was alleged that the Jews' fabulous wealth would enable them to buy all the land in England, take over Parliament and drive the English out. It was alleged, too, that the ministry had been bribed to pass the bill and that various unpopular groups (including deists and Papists) had promoted it in order to undermine the true Protestant religion. Such allegations were backed up by anti-semitic jibes about circumcision or the Crucifixion (93–5).[63]

The clamour against the bill was out of all proportion to its content, but it worked. Henry Pelham was not the man to take a stand on an issue of principle, especially with an election due in 1754. When Parliament reconvened the Act was repealed as quickly as it had been passed. From Pelham's point of view, his retreat was vindicated by the ministry's success in the election: Sir William Calvert, the bill's promoter, lost his seat (93). The Jews' legal position remained ill-defined but their disabilities were greater than those of Dissenters and Catholics. A campaign for emancipation in 1829–30 failed, but Jews were allowed to become freemen of the City and soon after they were allowed to acquire freehold land and be called to the bar. The Catholics gained emancipation because they were so numerous (in Ireland), but the Jews were few and had little popular support, so they remained the minority with the heaviest disabilities.[64]

III.
The Age of Reform
c.1780–1832

1. THE IMPACT OF THE INDUSTRIAL REVOLUTION

If the first half of the eighteenth century was a time of stability and complacency, the second saw rapid and profound changes. Industrial expansion earlier in the century had been based on villages rather than towns, with the normal unit of production the home rather than the factory. This old type of production persisted and expanded in many industries, but the late eighteenth century also saw the growth of factories and, with it, the concentration of industrial populations on an unprecedented scale. Such great social and economic changes created great problems for the churches. They created brutalised populations deprived of the framework of Christian values and instruction provided in rural parishes. Factory workers were more dependent and demoralised than the colliers and domestic handicraftsmen to whom Wesley and Whitefield had appealed. The mushrooming towns, unlike traditional villages, produced one-class communities, with no natural leaders or sense of identity. These developments posed difficulties for all denominations, but the Church found it especially hard to adapt to these shifts of population. The old parish system simply could not cope. The North, where the greatest urban expansion occurred, had always had too few parishes: there were only seventy in Lancashire, as against 731 in Norfolk.[65] As an Act of Parliament was needed to create a new parish, the Church would have found it far harder than other denominations to redeploy its resources, had it wished to do so. In fact, it showed only a limited interest in the new industrial masses. It had never accepted the logic of the loss of its monopoly position in 1689 and never appreciated the need to compete for adherents. Whenever possible, Churchmen fell back on legal harassment and ignored or deplored the changes which were taking place.

As a result of the prevailing attitude within the Church, the spiritual challenges of the early Industrial Revolution were met by others. Methodist numbers expanded rapidly, trebling between 1801 and 1831. They continued to open new chapels, but some of their initial momentum had been lost. Although they were still organised for expansion and although the hysterical element revived in some areas, there were within the movement growing pressures for consolidation. Established congregations (especially the wealthier members) preferred to channel their resources into fine new chapels rather than new missions elsewhere. These same wealthy laymen, as chapel trustees, wanted to clarify their legal status: itinerant preachers could not be licensed under the Toleration Act. They also pressed, successfully, for total separation from the Church of England. Gradually the Wesleyan Methodists lost their early doctrinal flexibility and willingness to co-operate with other Dissenters and became more introverted and denominationally minded. A series of secessions left the Wesleyan leadership more rigid, a tendency heightened by the dominance of the autocratic Jabez Bunting.[66]

As the Wesleyans paid more attention to consolidation, others took over the lead in the revival of evangelism to which the Methodists had given the initial impetus. Whether this revival was a continuation of the Wesleyan impulse, or a reaction against the French Revolution, or a response to social change, it had a massive impact on English life from the 1780s. The Primitive Methodists rediscovered the spontaneity and excitement which the Wesleyans had largely lost. They brought to England the American 'camp meeting', a religious event lasting several days which sustained a high level of excitement. As Wesleyanism became dominated by the clergy and wealthy laity, Primitive Methodism remained essentially working-class and was unusual in mounting successful missions to the industrial poor.[67] There were similar developments among some other sects. The Quakers remained introverted and their numbers continued to decline. English Presbyterianism was moribund and was to revive only as a result of Scots immigration. Most Presbyterians had by now become Unitarians, too intellectual and too radical in politics to attract much support. Joseph Priestley, a distinguished chemist and Unitarian minister, welcomed the French Revolution and agitated for political reform. His house, and those of some of his supporters, were wrecked by 'Church and king' mobs in 1791 (96–7). After the conservative reaction of the 1790s, Unitarianism survived as only a minor denomination.[68]

If Quakers and Presbyterians failed to adapt to changing circumstances, others did. Inspired, perhaps, by the Methodists' success, a new generation of Congregationalists and Baptists reacted against the rigid and arid Calvinism of the Old Dissent. They wanted more emotion in religion and set out to preach in a way that the poor and uneducated could understand. They avoided esoteric theological points and concentrated on basic questions of salvation and damnation. Concerned with the heart rather than the head, they sometimes generated collective hysteria, as with the 'Jumpers', in Wales, who jumped in unison during sermons. The events of the 1790s revived millenarian enthusiasms. It seemed that Rome might fall at last and some hoped that the Jews might be converted or the French become Protestants: a Dr Coke set off for Paris, but returned disappointed. The missionary effect within England was far more successful. Four times as many Dissenting meeting houses were registered in the 1790s as in the 1770s. The Baptists and Congregationalists imitated the Methodists' use of itinerancy and lay preachers. Like the early Methodists, they concentrated on conversion and expansion. There was much local co-operation between denominations in the organisation of preaching and the opening of Sunday schools. These multiplied greatly in the late eighteenth century and were in part an attempt to keep poor children out of trouble on Sundays: the New Dissent shared the traditional Puritan concern for moral discipline. To the Methodists these schools could eradicate at an early age the sin inherent in human nature: 'Break their wills betimes . . . if you would not damn the child', wrote Wesley. The revival's greatest appeal was not to disoriented factory workers but to independent or semi-independent craftsmen and shopkeepers, especially in the extended parishes of pastoral regions, where parson and squire wielded less influence than in the nucleated arable villages of the South-East.[69]

Between 1780 and 1820 the churches enjoyed their greatest expansion since at least the mid-seventeenth century, yet that expansion went unnoted in the popular prints, except for wideranging satires on 'the progress of cant' (*105–6*) or traditional satires on hell-fire preachers (*120*). This omission owed nothing to censorship, which had disappeared, but reflected market forces: print-makers did not think they could sell prints of proletarian Baptists preaching to unwashed villagers. For the revival to be commercially interesting, it had to be scandalous or ridiculous. Sophisticated Londoners mocked those taken in by the prophecies of Joanna Southcott (*98–9*), a Devon woman who proclaimed that only those who received her 'seals' would be saved and, in 1814, that she would give birth to a new messiah. In the gloom and hardship of the Napoleonic Wars such prophets (like the emotionalism of Primitive Methodists and rural Ranters) offered a glimmer of hope to the downtrodden. Here, amid desolation, was the consolation of individual salvation – the 'chiliasm of despair'.[70]

If it is understandable that print-makers ignored the Protestant revival, it is surprising that they also ignored the rapid growth of Catholicism. The 1791 Relief Act allowed priests to preach and minister freely, just as the growth of the cities opened up a new field for missionary activity. With their strong discipline, based on the confessional, and pastoral care, the Catholics were well equipped to win and hold converts. Urban Catholicism expanded rapidly. Much of this was due to Irish immigration, but many of these new Catholics were English.[71] Thus English Catholicism began to lose its aristocratic and rural ethos and became far more working-class and urban, a development ignored by the prints.

2. THE IMPACT OF THE FRENCH REVOLUTION

For much of the seventeenth and eighteenth centuries, while the religious convictions of many were lukewarm or minimal, few openly attacked revealed religion. Religion was an integral part of a social and political order which few were prepared to challenge. From the 1760s this cosy consensus began to break down. Some, like Tom Paine, denounced not only particular faults of the existing political system but the system itself. The Americans' success in establishing, from scratch, a more liberal and equal political system led many to demand similar changes in Britain. The Americans, moreover, set up a state without an established church. This strengthened the arguments of those demanding full civil and political rights for religious minorities and also those, like Paine, who questioned whether organised religion was necessary at all. Paine was a deist, not an atheist; he argued that churches stunted intellectual development by filling men's heads with irrelevant fables and maintaining a stranglehold on education. They also maintained a useless, expensive and parasitic body of clergy. Religious and political radicals initially welcomed the French Revolution as overthrowing a corrupt and authoritarian monarchy and an obscurantist and authoritarian church. They celebrated the fall of the Bastille and expressed hopes of similar developments within Britain.

The radicals received scant sympathy from the print-makers who catered for a market more affluent than that of the radical journalists. As the Revolution moved from liberal reform to republicanism, deism and military expansion, so the radicals came to appear dangerous. Anxious conservatives looked to religion to buttress the existing order. They claimed that Christianity was an integral feature of the existing constitution and so works of 'blasphemy' (like Paine's *Age of Reason*) were harassed as much as works of 'sedition'. The rulers of society struck back at the radicals in various ways – legal harassment, 'Church and king' mobs, counter-propaganda like the *Anti-Jacobin Magazine* (100). With the start of the war against France, conservatives also appealed to patriotism as the radicals were identified with a hostile power. By 1795 the radicals' chance had passed, if it had ever existed, but with the post-war slump and disillusionment came a degree of social and political antagonism unprecedented in England. Some revived the arguments and publications of the 1790s: Richard Carlile was jailed on a charge of blasphemous libel for republishing Paine's works (101). Others extended the attack on revealed religion. To Shelley, virtue was inherent in man and could be developed through knowledge and education, through the 'march of mind'. Morality was thus intellectual rather than spiritual and its development was impeded by the clergy who, for their own selfish interests, kept the people deluded and ignorant (102, 105–6). Here was a concept of human progress in which religion had no place. It could lead, as with Carlile, to arguments for total freedom of expression. It could also, with the Benthamites, justify schemes of social engineering, whereby the 'right' values were to be inculcated through a carefully controlled educational system.[72]

The arguments against organised religion which developed after 1815 appealed to a wider audience, thanks to cheap newspapers and pamphlets, illustrated with simple woodcuts, aimed at a far less affluent market than the expensive and sophisticated prints. After Peterloo, with fears of revolution in the air, sceptics and unbelievers seemed to threaten the foundations of the old order (101, 103–4). In 1818–20 the government managed to intimidate some radical publishers and journalists by a series of prosecutions, but far more radical prints appeared in the 1820s than in the 1790s, perhaps in part because political radicalism was no longer linked with the threat of foreign invasion. Most radical satirists, moreover, attacked not revealed religion but the Church of England, now increasingly identified with the unreformed political order.

3. THE CHURCH OF ENGLAND

Before 1780 there had been many satires on the Church, but most were mild and good-natured. After about 1780 there appeared an element of bitterness and hostility. No longer was the Church an accepted institution whose abuses were, at worst, mildly irritating. Many now thought it so corrupt that it needed to be drastically reformed or even disestablished. In part, this change was just another example of an increasingly radical and questioning attitude, seen also in demands for political reform and attacks on organized religion, but certain developments within the Church led its critics to single it out for special condemnation.

In the later eighteenth century the price of food rose substantially. This meant bigger profits for producers and a larger income for those clergymen who received their tithes in kind. A spate of enclosure acts redistributed the land in many villages on a more rational basis. Often those involved took the chance to free their land of tithe by awarding the parson a share of the land – perhaps one seventh – in lieu of tithe. With the boom in agricultural prices, such awards proved very profitable. Many clergymen, especially in the south east, came to enjoy a much larger income. Socially and economically they moved nearer to the gentry than to their own parishioners. Some claimed their parsonages were too small and decrepit to match up to their enhanced status, so lived elsewhere, perhaps employing the usual underpaid curate: non-residence increased in the early nineteenth century. The growing social gulf between priests and people was often widened by lawsuits about tithe and other property matters. With the slump in farm prices after 1815, those clergymen whose tithes had been commuted for a cash payment tried to exact the full amount from farmers struggling to make ends meet. There were many reasons why (in Cobbett's words) the labouring people's 'way of thinking and feeling with regard to both Church and clergy are totally changed and there is now very little moral hold which the latter possess'.[73] Another consequence of the 'gentrification' of many parsons was a growing number of clerical J.P.s. By the 1820s a quarter of J.P.s were clergymen and one parson in eight was on the bench. This bound the clergy still more closely to the aristocratic social and political order. Most clergymen uncritically defended the existing ecclesiastical order, with all its anomalies, thus laying themselves open to attacks whose motivation was political as well as religious.[74]

The most basic object of criticism was tithe. The clergy were denounced as greedy (*108, 111*), imposing an intolerable burden on landowner and farmer (*107*). In the age of 'economical reform', when the political use of places and sinecures was denounced, some of the inequalities in the Church were too gross to escape censure. The rector of Stanhope received £4,843 per annum, of which he paid £270 to curates. The bishop of Durham, his revenues swollen by royalties from coalmining, was said to receive more than eighty-four French bishops put together (*115*). The increase in clerical incomes heightened criticism of such abuses and of the Church's pastoral failings. The wealth of many churchmen also contrasted sharply with the hardships of working people during and after the Napoleonic Wars (*109*). Small wonder, it was argued, that the clergy had a vested interest in opposing reform (*110*). While not neglecting the Church's spiritual and pastoral failings (*115–6*), its critics' complaints were increasingly political. They denounced ultra-conservative clerical J.P.s (*112*) and depicted the Church as part of a monstrous and impossibly burdensome establishment sustained by the systematic misuse of the law and, failing that, by armed force (112–4). As one journalist wrote in 1820 of the chapter of Durham, which was both very rich and very conservative:

> *It is impossible that such a system can last. It is at war with the spirit of the age, as well as with justice and reason, and the beetles who crawl about amidst its holes and crevices act as if they were striving to provoke and accelerate the blow which, sooner or later, will inevitably crush the whole fabric, and level it with the dust.*[75]

Although the Church usually ignored criticism, it was not wholly immune from the spirit of reform. The spirit of evangelism, revived by the Methodists, strongly influenced a minority of churchmen. Like Wesley, these Evangelicals stressed the value of the liturgy and of communion, but their main concerns were conversion and moral improvement. They stressed the broad moral and spiritual content of religion rather than particular doctrines, rather like the earlier Puritans: most Evangelicals were, in fact, Calvinists. They were ready to co-operate informally with Dissenters who were tackling similar problems in a similar way. Like many Dissenters, they saw the answers to the social and political problems created by the Industrial and French Revolutions mainly in moral and spiritual terms. They saw society sliding into vice, crime and anarchy and sought a remedy in religious education, through preaching, Sunday schools, societies for moral improvement and more diligent pastoral care: by this they meant not only regular sermons and communion, but also such ancillary activities as prayer-meetings and Bible-classes. Whatever the Dissenters achieved, only the Church, with its parish system, possessed a framework for nationwide moral regeneration. To Anglican reformers the first priority was to revive the parish system, by enforcing residence, improving clerical standards and (where necessary) building new churches. Within the Church, these calls for reform bore little fruit. The tangle of vested interests surrounding clerical preferments made a major improvement of clerical standards very difficult. Moreover, many of the hierarchy were suspicious of the Evangelicals' links with Dissenters. It is perhaps significant that the most important reform of the early nineteenth century was the work of a mainly High Church pressure group. In 1818 Parliament set up a Church Building Commission with funds of a million pounds, later increased. In the next forty years this body promoted the building of some six hundred churches, usually with the help of voluntary subscriptions. The style of the new churches was not always popular – Cobbett called them 'heaps of white rubbish that the parsons have late stuck up . . . built with money forced from the nation by odious taxes' (*125–6*) – but they marked the Church's first positive response to the Industrial Revolution.[76]

If the Evangelicals failed to regenerate the Church, their influence on society was considerable. They organised crusades against vice and profanity (*119*) and against the slave trade and the more glaring sufferings caused by early industrialism. Even more important, they helped restore a sense of moral seriousness to the upper classes. Their aim was 'to do within the Church and nearer the throne what Wesley has done in the meeting and among the multitude', to 'cleanse the high places of the land'. They reminded the aristocracy that religion could serve a valuable social purpose, as it 'renders the inequalities of the civil state less galling to the lower orders'. They also helped restore an element of moral decency, even piety, to public life. The Victorians were apt to treat religion more seriously than most eighteenth-century politicians had done.[77]

If this was the Evangelicals' greatest achievement, they were prevented from achieving more within the Church by their limited number and isolation. They were less successful than Dissenters and Methodists in reaching the bulk of the urban population, although, like them, the Church participated in the expansion of Sunday schooling from the 1780s. Like the Wesleyans, Churchmen saw schools as instruments of social discipline in a society which was losing its old values. In rural areas, the Anglican schools programme was a success: only six Oxfordshire villages lacked schools in 1838. In such areas, however, the Church faced little competition. In the towns, the Wesleyan schools in particular proved more successful than those of the Church. By 1811 there were two rival school societies, one non-denominational (but identified with Dissent) and one Anglican (*121–2*). The supporters of Church schools denounced those of their opponents as godless. They used similar arguments against London University (later University College), which deliberately eschewed theology, and founded King's College to counteract its influence (*123–4*).[78]

In education, where its legal privileges were limited, the Church had no choice but to compete. In general, it preferred to cling to its legal advantages. Anglican J.P.s harassed Methodists and Dissenters. Parliament refused to remove the legal disabilities on Dissenters (*117*) and even considered further measures against them. By 1815, however, the Dissenters' legal position had been strengthened and they had acquired friends even in the royal family (*118*). The Churchmen's conduct might have been realistic had the Church still possessed reserves of power in its own right. As it depended entirely on the secular state, it was dangerous for so many of the clergy to take an extreme and possibly unpopular line in politics, thus making themselves vulnerable on political as well as ecclesiastical grounds, for there was always a danger that their lay allies might abandon them in a crisis. Their reactionary conduct after Peterloo, in fact, ensured that the Church would be criticised as much as the unreformed Parliament.

4. CATHOLIC EMANCIPATION AND THE CRISIS OF 1828–32

The Toleration Act left the Church in a position that was ambivalent in theory and still more uncertain in practice. Protestant Dissenters (except Unitarians) could worship freely, but the Test and Corporation Acts remained in force and should have excluded them from public office. Between 1791 and 1813 freedom of worship was extended to Catholics and Unitarians and the legal position of Methodism was secured. Dissenters remained excluded from office, but that exclusion was tempered by occasional conformity and by a series of temporary indemnity acts, dispensing them from the need to take the Test. English Catholics were excluded from offices, from Parliament and from voting in elections, although Irish Catholic freeholders could vote from 1793.[79] Thus while the Church had lost all claim to direct the spiritual life of a large part of the nation, its politically privileged position was precariously preserved, until 1828–9. Then both Dissenters and Catholics were granted virtually full political and civil rights. Even then, Dissenters were still obliged by law to pay tithes and church rates and to be married in a parish church.

In 1787–90 the Dissenters failed in three attempts to have the Test and Corporation Acts repealed. The fears aroused by the French Revolution made it easy to see this as part of a dastardly plot to overthrow the established order in church and state (*131–2*).[80] Where the Dissenters failed, the Catholics succeeded, with the Relief Act of 1791: politically (for once) the Catholics did not seem dangerous. By 1828 the position had changed. The repeal of the laws affecting Dissenters was now far less contentious than the repeal of those affecting Catholics. The Dissenters had no alien connotations and, although some still claimed that Dissenters were subversive, this was hard to sustain in the face of the cautious and conservative utterances of their leaders. The Methodist Conference claimed credit for 'raising the standard of public morals and promoting loyalty in the middle ranks as well as subordination and industry in the lower orders of society'. 'Methodism hates democracy as much as it hates sin,' declared Bunting.[81] The most radical denomination, the Unitarians, had declined since the 1790s. The Catholics, by contrast, still seemed alien, subjects of the pope rather than the king. The French wars had led some to qualify their dislike of Popery. Catholic refugees from France were well received. Propagandists were sometimes prepared to treat Catholics (even priests and nuns) sympathetically, provided they were hostile to France (*128*). The Catholic question was then transformed by the Union with Ireland. In the 1790s the British government feared that Ireland might revolt or be 'liberated' by the French (*127*) and so pushed through the Union of 1800. This ensured that the Irish Catholics' campaign for civil and political equality would now be directed towards Westminster and that traditional English dislike of the Irish would add an extra element to anti-Popery. 'The English do not dislike us as Catholics, they simply hate us as Irish,' declared Daniel O'Connell.[82]

In promoting the Union Pitt had virtually promised the Catholics emancipation, but George III would not let him keep his promise and he resigned. In this, the king was in agreement with the majority in both Houses and with public opinion. A Catholic petition to Parliament in 1805 was firmly rejected (*133–5*). The king's ministers still hoped to do something for the Catholics and proposed that they should be admitted to all ranks of the army. George refused to agree and the ministry resigned (*136*). The new Tory ministry was hostile to emancipation. It was prepared to consider an emancipation bill in 1813 only on condition that the government should exercise some control over clerical appointments and that Catholic priests and office-holders should swear a special oath of temporal allegiance to the king, thus meeting the objection that Catholics were primarily subjects of the pope. Most English lay Catholics were ready to accept these conditions (or 'securities'), but the Irish clergy were not and the bill was withdrawn (*137*).[83]

Irish M.P.s sympathetic to emancipation continued to raise the question, but not until 1821 was permission given to bring in another bill. The ministry was divided and gave no 'official' lead. The bill passed the Commons (thanks to substantial provision for 'securities'), but was rejected by the Lords, led by Lord Eldon and George IV's brother and heir, the Duke of York (*138–9*). The rejection aroused mixed feelings in Ireland. Many Catholics had been unhappy about the 'securities' but the rejection encouraged the proponents of emancipation to extend the scope of their campaign. In 1823 Daniel O'Connell, a Catholic lawyer, founded the Catholic Association to press for emancipation and to promote Catholic interests in general. With a subscription of a penny a month and the support of many priests, it attracted vast numbers of adherents and turned the emancipation campaign into a mass movement. In the minds of many adherents, it also extended the campaign's scope. For Irish Catholics (unlike the English) religious disabilities formed only a part of a complex of deprivations and resentments – agrarian, social, political, nationalistic. The Association raised hopes that all the grievances would be remedied and, perhaps, that the Union would be dissolved and Ireland become self-governing.[84]

The founding of the Catholic Association alarmed the British government, since it created virtually an alternative government in Ireland: its committee was nicknamed the 'Popish Parliament' (*140*). An attempt to suppress the Association by statute failed, as O'Connell revived it under another name. With the mass support provided by the Association, the Irish Catholics were no longer supplicants but bargained from a position of power: eventually they got their way because they were able – and apparently willing – to plunge Ireland into chaos. That point had not yet been reached in 1825 when O'Connell promoted a bill to grant emancipation, with certain securities. It provoked several hundred hostile petitions and, as in 1821, passed the Commons but was rejected in the Lords, where York declared that the king could not assent to it without violating his coronation oath (*141*).[85]

As frustration and violence increased in Ireland, the ministry was divided, with Canning in favour of emancipation and York and Eldon against (*143–4*). Both York and Canning died in 1827 which led George IV, eventually, to turn to Wellington. Wellington and Peel, his lieutenant in the Commons, had hitherto opposed emancipation but were pragmatic enough to accept that, given the condition of Ireland, it could not long be denied. In 1828 Wellington agreed to the repeal of the Test and Corporation Acts, insofar as they applied to Protestants. This did not destroy the principle of the 'Protestant constitution' but provided a precedent (which the Catholics were quick to use) for undermining the Church's politically privileged position. By now, however, argument counted for less than the threat of force. In July 1828 O'Connell (although as a Catholic ineligible to sit in Parliament) won a by-election in County Clare. This raised the spectre of Catholics being elected in many Irish constituencies in the next general election. If they were then excluded from Parliament, they would presumably set up their own assembly, which would surely precipitate a war of independence. To preserve the Union, Wellington had to grant emancipation, but first he had to win over the king and Lords. George IV was less strong-minded than his father, but nursed occasional febrile visions of reviving the lost powers of the crown. Wellington had to lead and bully him and cope with his constant changes of heart. 'The old fool, sometimes tormented by gout, at others stupefied by laudanum, would not come to any decision,' grumbled the Duke. The king's obstinacy was encouraged by some Tories, who urged him to use his veto, and by anti-Catholic agitation outside Parliament. At last Wellington convinced the king that he had no choice. With king and cabinet committed to emancipation, the Lords yielded and the bill passed in April 1829 (*146, 148*).[86]

The bill's final draft included few of the 'securities' which the government had once thought necessary, although it disfranchised the poorest Irish freeholders and outlawed the Catholic Association. Catholics were excluded from a few offices, including lord chancellor of England. O'Connell thought the terms 'very good; frank, direct, complete'.[87] In law, at least, British and Irish Catholics were no longer second-class citizens. Although some argued that popular anti-Popery sprang from ignorance and misrepresentation (*142, 145*), the British public was clearly mainly hostile to emancipation, a fact reflected in the prints. However, the public's resentment was not so intense that it was ready to use violence to prevent the bill's taking effect. Its attention was soon diverted to the questions of parliamentary reform and the implications of emancipation for the Church of England.

For those who saw a Protestant established church as an integral part of the constitution, who believed that Church and state had evolved as a single organic growth, emancipation signalled the death of the constitution (*147*).[88] Meanwhile, sensing that the Church could no longer count on the ministry's protection, its enemies closed in for the kill (*149*). Dissenters and radicals demanded that it should be disestablished and that church rates (for the upkeep of parish churches) and tithes should be abolished. The Extraordinary Black Book of 1831 painted a highly coloured, but basically accurate, picture of widespread pluralism, non-residence and pastoral neglect. It was easy to argue that many clergymen, especially in cathedral chapters, served no useful purpose and that Church revenues should be taken over by the state and put to better use (*150, 154*).

Although the Church made some concessions on tithe, its basic reaction was to rely on the protection of Parliament. Most of the clergy opposed parliamentary reform, which made their position still more precarious. Severe economic depression led to a serious breakdown of order in rural areas, including violent refusals to pay tithe, while the parliamentary reform agitation resumed with added vehemence. Only two bishops voted for reform in 1831 and twenty-one against: had all the bishops voted for the reform bill, it would have passed the Lords. The bishops were blamed for the bill's failure and the 1831 general election saw many cases of violence against the clergy: the Bishop of Bristol's palace was burned down. Lord Grey, the Whig minister who had promoted the bill, had warned the bishops of the consquences of their action and was not displeased at their discomfiture (*151–2*). After Wellington had failed to form a new ministry, Grey returned. Faced with a threat to create new peers if necessary, most of the bishops and other Tories dropped their opposition and the bill passed in June 1832.[89]

When the Reform Bill passed it seemed to many that 'the Church, as it now stands, no human power can save' (*153*).[90] In fact, the Whig ministry of 1832–4 was too weak to undertake radical church reform and Peel's return to office in 1834 gave the Church a friend in the ministry. Meanwhile, the Church digested and applied the lessons of 1828–32. No longer could it rely on its lay friends to protect its privileges. It had to stand on its own feet and compete with other denominations. To do this it had to adopt their techniques of petitioning, lobbying and propaganda, but it had also to overcome its pastoral failings in order to compete at the parish level. 'The people must be gained', wrote Bishop Blomfield, 'or all is lost'. Utility and efficiency became the order of the day. The church-building programme was accelerated. A first step was taken towards the more rational use of church resources, with a redistribution of the revenues of bishops and chapters. The founding of the Ecclesiastical Commission gave the Church a central policy-making body for the first time since the effective disappearance of Convocation. Most important, the parish clergy attended to their duties far more assiduously than before, an improvement which in many cases had started before 1828. Non-residence was much reduced. The clergy extended their responsibilities to include certain 'social services': education, coal and clothing clubs, libraries. This enabled the Church to strengthen its position in rural parishes, although it remained weak in working-class areas of industrial towns. The number of practising Anglicans increased greatly: in terms of numbers the Church regained much of the ground it had lost before 1832, while the expansion of Methodism and Dissent slowed down. There remained vast inequalities of income within the Church and its preferments were still entangled in an intricate web of vested interests. The right of presentation to about half of England's parishes remained in lay hands. Even so, the Church regained sufficient vitality to resist pressures for disestablishment. For a while, too, Oxford and Cambridge remained wholly Anglican. Since 1600 English Protestantism had divided and redivided and English Catholics had emerged from persecution and proscription. Yet the Church of England had survived, in a somewhat muddled and anomalous fashion, an established church, without coercive powers and with limited and diminishing privileges, in a world of religious pluralism.[91]

FOOTNOTES

1. F. Siebert, *Freedom of the Press in England, 1476–1776* (Urbana, 1952), chs. 13, 18; A. Aspinall, *Politics and the Press, 1780–1850* (London, 1949), ch. 2; M. D. George, *English Political Caricature* (2 vols., Oxford, 1959), I, pp. 2–3, 122.
2. An exception is Hogarth's 'Transubstantiation Satirised' (77).
3. Of over 17,000 prints in the British Library collection for the period up to 1832, less than ten per cent date from before 1714.
4. J. L. Waddy, *The Bitter Sacred Cup: The Wednesbury Riots, 1743–4* (World Methodist Historical Society, 1976), p. 12; R. B. Rose, 'The Priestley Riots of 1791', *Past and Present*, no. 18 (1960), pp. 72–3; J. Miller, *Popery and Politics in England, 1660–88* (Cambridge, 1973), ch. 4.
5. E. P. Thompson, *The Making of the English Working Class* (Harmondsworth, 1968), pp. 77, 39n.
6. See E. R. Norman, *Anti-Catholicism in Victorian England* (London, 1968).
7. See P. Collinson, *The Elizabethan Puritan Movement* (London, 1967).
8. See N. Tyacke, 'Puritanism, Arminianism and Counter-Revolution', in C. Russell (ed.), *Origins of the English Civil War* (London, 1973).
9. Article XVII; see also W. Haller, *The Rise of Puritanism* (New York, 1938), pp. 83–91, 215.
10. H. Davies, *Worship and Theology in England: II. 1603–90* (Princeton, 1975) p. 13.
11. A. Fletcher, *A County Community in Peace and War: Sussex 1600–60* (London, 1975), pp. 86–93; P. Clark, *English Provincial Society from the Reformation to the Revolution: Kent 1500–1640* (Hassocks, 1977), pp. 361–9.
12. S. R. Gardiner, *History of England, 1603–42* (10 vols., London, 1883-4), IX, p. 278; S. R. Gardiner, *Constitutional Documents of the Puritan Revolution, 1625–60* (3rd edn., Oxford, 1951), p. 216; see also R. Clifton, 'Fear of Popery' in Russell (ed.), *Origins of the English Civil War*, ch. 5.
13. Gardiner, *History of England*, IX, pp. 276–87, 386–90, X, pp. 39–41.
14. R. S. Paul, *The Lord Protector* (London, 1955), p. 25.
15. J. F. Wilson, *Pulpit in Parliament* (Princeton, 1969); W. M. Lamont, *Godly Rule: Politics and Religion 1603–60* (London, 1969), pp. 79–84, 93–8.
16. G. F. Nuttall, *Visible Saints: The Congregational Way, 1640–60* (Oxford, 1957), p. 54. On Independency in general, see Nuttall, passim and M. Tolmie, *The Triumph of the Saints: The Separate Churches of London 1616–49* (Cambridge, 1977), pp. 28–34, 96–8, 100–1, 116–19.
17. Nuttall, *Visible Saints*, pp. 110–23 (quotation from p. 116); A. S. P. Woodhouse, *Puritanism and Liberty: The Army Debates 1647–9* (London, 1938), p. 97.
18. Nuttall, *Visible Saints*, pp. 123–30, 148–53, 156–8 and passim; Paul, *Lord Protector*, pp. 328–30.
19. Gardiner, *Documents*, p. 268; see also R. Ashton, *The English Civil War, 1603–49* (London, 1978), pp. 202–3.
20. V. Pearl, 'London Puritans and Scotch Fifth Columnists', in A. E. J. Hollaender and W. Kellaway (eds.), *Studies in London History Presented to P. E.*

Jones (London, 1969), pp. 317–31; V. Pearl, 'Exorcist or Historian: The Dangers of Ghost-Hunting', *Past and Present*, no. 47 (1970), pp. 125–7; C. G. Bolam, J. J. Goring, H. L. Short and R. Thomas, *The English Presbyterians* (London, 1968), pp. 38–45.

21. Gardiner, *History of England*, IX, p. 285.
22. Bolam, Goring, Short and Thomas, *Presbyterians*, pp. 19–21, 34–8, 46–60.
23. C. Hill, *The World Turned Upside Down* (Harmondsworth, 1975), p. 215 and ch. 9 passim. See also A. L. Morton, *The World of the Ranters* (London, 1970).
24. Hill, *World Turned Upside Down*, ch. 10.
25. W. C. Abbott, *Writings and Speeches of Oliver Cromwell* (4 vols., Cambridge, Mass., 1929–47), II, p. 339.
26. On the Church in the 1650s, see S. R. Gardiner, *History of the Great Civil War* (4 vols., London, 1893), III, pp. 199–203; S. R. Gardiner, *History of the Commonwealth and Protectorate* (4 vols., London, 1903), II, pp. 84–102, III, pp. 19–27; G. R. Abernathy, 'The English Presbyterians and the Stuart Restoration, 1648– 63', *Transactions of the American Philosophical Society*, LV. (1965), pp. 6–17; C. Cross, 'The Church in England, 1646–60', in G. E. Aylmer (ed.), *The Interregnum* (London, 1972), ch. 4.
27. Fletcher, *Sussex*, p. 113.
28. cf. the quotations in C. H. Firth, *Oliver Cromwell and the Rule of the Puritans in England* (London, 1953), p. 411; J. T. Rutt (ed.), *Diary of Thomas Burton* (4 vols., 1828), I, p. 281.
29. Davies, *Worship and Theology*, II, p. 365.
30. See I. M. Green, *The Re-Establishment of the Church of England* (Oxford, 1978); A. Whiteman, 'The Restoration of the Church of England' and R. Thomas, 'Comprehension and Indulgence', both in G. F. Nuttall and O. Chadwick (eds.), *From Uniformity to Unity, 1662–1962* (London, 1962); R. Beddard, 'The Restoration Church' in J. R. Jones (ed.), *The Restored Monarchy, 1660–88* (London, 1979), ch. 7.
31. N. Sykes, *From Sheldon to Secker* (Cambridge, 1959), pp. 28–9; A. F. W. Papillon, *Memoirs of Thomas Papillon* (Reading, 1887), pp. 374–6.
32. N. Sykes, *Church and State in England in the Eighteenth Century* (Cambridge, 1934), pp. 256–72; Sykes, *Sheldon to Secker*, pp. 142–53, 176–87; G. R. Cragg, *From Puritanism to the Age of Reason* (Cambridge, 1950), chs. 2–4.
33. See Miller, *Popery and Politics*, ch. 8.
34. Lord Braybrooke (ed.), *Autobiography of Sir John Bramston* (Camden Society, 1845), p. 338.
35. On the Church under William and Anne see G. V. Bennett, *The Tory Crisis in Church and State, 1688–1730* (Oxford, 1975); G. V. Bennett, 'Conflict in the Church' in G. Holmes (ed.), *Britain After the Glorious Revolution* (London 1969), ch. 7; G. Holmes, *The Trial of Dr Sacheverell* (London, 1973), ch. 2.
36. See J. P. Kenyon, *Revolution Principles: The Politics of Party, 1689–1720* (Cambridge, 1977).
37. J. Wickham Legg, *English Church Life from the Restoration to the Tractarian Movement* (London, 1914), p. 9; on the trial and the riots, see Holmes, *Sacheverell*; G. Holmes, 'The Sacheverell Riots', *Past and Present*, no. 72 (1976), pp. 55–85. See also George, *English Caricature*, I. 68.
38. Sykes, *Church and State*, pp. 275–82.
39. Sykes, *Church and State*, p. 231.
40. Sykes, *Church and State*, pp. 215–20; A. D. Gilbert, *Religion and Society in Industrial England, 1740–1914* (London, 1976), p. 7.
41. Sykes, *Church and State*, pp. 185–6.

42. Sykes, *Church and State*, pp. 206–20; G. F. A. Best, *Temporal Pillars: Queen Anne's Bounty, the Ecclesiastical Commissioners and the Church of England* (Cambridge, 1964), pp. 13–18; Gilbert, *Religion and Society*, pp. 5–6; A. Warne, *Church and Society in Eighteenth-Century Devon* (Newton Abbot, 1969), pp. 38–42; D. McClatchey, *Oxfordshire Clergy, 1777–1869* (Oxford, 1960), pp. 32–46, 71–5.
43. Sykes, *Church and State*, p. 157.
44. M. G. Jones, *The Charity School Movement* (Cambridge, 1938); G. Williams, *Religion, Language and Nationality in Wales* (Cardiff, 1979), ch. 9.
45. N. Sykes, *Edmund Gibson* (Oxford, 1926), pp. 133–75; Best, *Temporal Pillars*, pp. 37–44, 59–61, 93–108.
46. Wickham Legg, *Church Life*, pp. 121–5; A. Armstrong, *The Church of England, the Methodists and Society, 1700–1850* (London, 1973), pp. 30–3.
47. Warne, *Devon*, p. 50. See also Cobbett's remark: 'The working clergy of the Church of England are . . . as good men as any in the world': N. Gash, *Aristocracy and People, 1815–65* (London, 1979), p. 60.
48. Bolam, Goring, Short and Thomas, *Presbyterians*, pp. 130–74; Gilbert, *Religion and Society*, pp. 15–7; Armstrong, *Church, Methodists and Society*, pp. 35–42; Thompson, *Working Class*, pp. 31–8.
49. H. Davies, *Worship and Theology in England: III. 1690–1850* (Princeton, 1961), p. 147.
50. R. E. Davies and E. G. Rupp (eds.), *History of the Methodist Church in Great Britain: I. The Eighteenth Century* (London, 1965), p. 57.
51. J. D. Walsh, 'Origins of the Evangelical Revival', in G. V. Bennett and J. D. Walsh (eds.), *Essays in Modern English Church History in Memory of Norman Sykes* (London, 1966), p. 149.
52. Bolam, Goring, Short and Thomas, *Presbyterians*, p. 218; Thompson, *Working Class*, p. 31.
53. Davies and Rupp (eds.), *Methodist Church*, I, p. 54.
54. Waddy, *Bitter Sacred Cup*, passim.
55. Davies and Rupp (eds.), *Methodist Church*, I, pp. 147–67; Thompson, *Working Class*, p. 41; Armstrong, *Church, Methodists and Society*, pp. 81–3, 105.
56. Armstrong, *Church, Methodists and Society*, p. 112.
57. Armstrong, *Church, Methodists and Society*, p. 66; see also Davies and Rupp (eds.), *Methodist Church*, I, pp. 213–55.
58. N. Rogers, 'Popular Protest in Early Hanoverian London', *Past and Present*, no. 79 (1978), pp. 70–100.
59. G. Rudé, 'The Gordon Riots', *Transactions of the Royal Historical Society*, 5th Series, VI (1956), pp. 95–108; G. Rudé, *The Crowd in History, 1730–1848* (New York, 1964), pp. 57–60.
60. Rudé, 'Gordon Riots', pp. 106–13; Thompson, *Working Class*, pp. 77–8; George, *English Caricature*, I, p. 143.
61. E. Halévy, *History of the English People in the Nineteenth Century: I. England in 1815* (London, 1949), pp. 478–9; U. Henriques, *Religious Toleration in England, 1787–1833* (London, 1961), p. 137; E. I. Watkin, *Roman Catholicism in England* (London, 1957), pp. 131–8, 144–8.
62. Gardiner, *Commonwealth*, IV, pp. 10-8; T. W. Perry, *Public Opinion, Propaganda and Politics in 18th Century England: The Jew Bill of 1753* (Cambridge, Mass., 1962), pp. 5–8; M. D. George, *London Life in the Eighteenth Century* (Harmondsworth, 1966), pp. 131–6.
63. See Perry, *Public Opinion*, passim.
64. Henriques, *Religious Toleration*, pp. 179–91.

65. W. R. Ward, *Religion and Society in England, 1790–1850* (London, 1972), p. 108.
66. Davies and Rupp (eds.), *Methodist Church*, I, pp. 279–315; Gilbert, *Religion and Society*, pp. 30–2; Thompson, *Working Class*, pp. 417–19; Ward, *Religion and Society*, pp. 85–104, 135–67.
67. Armstrong, *Church, Methodists and Society*, pp. 199–213; Ward, *Religion and Society*, pp. 75–83.
68. Rose, 'Priestley Riots'.
69. Davies and Rupp (eds.), *Methodist Church*, I, pp. 296–302; Halévy, *English People*, I, pp. 419–20; Gilbert, *Religion and Society*, pp. 32–43, 51–67, 94–114; Ward, *Religion and Society*, pp. 12–16, 44–50; Thompson, *Working Class*, p. 412 (quoted).
70. Thompson, *Working Class*, pp. 420–6.
71. J. Bossy, *The English Catholic Community, 1570–1850* (London, 1975), ch. 13.
72. George, *English Caricature*, I, pp. 220–1; Henriques, *Religious Toleration*, pp. 206–7, 236–8; Thompson, *Working Class*, pp. 105–7.
73. W. Cobbett, *Rural Rides* (2 vols., Every-man edn., n.d.), I, p. 226; see also *ibid.*, I, pp. 120–1, 180–1, II, pp. 60, 123–4, 266.
74. W. R. Ward, 'The Tithe Question in England in the Early Nineteenth Century', *Journal of Ecclesiastical History*, XVI. (1965), pp. 67–81; Ward, *Religion and Society*, pp. 9–12, 112-24; Best, *Temporal Pillars*, pp. 62–75; McClatchey, *Oxfordshire Clergy*, pp. 97–120.
75. Best, *Temporal Pillars*, p. 247n.; see also Cobbett, *Rural Rides*, I, pp. 209–10.
76. Davies, *Worship and Theology*, III, pp. 217–31; Armstrong, *Church, Methodists and Society*, pp. 125–30, 176–83; Best, *Temporal Pillars*, pp. 137–47; M. H. Port, *Six Hundred New Churches: The Church Building Commission, 1818–56* (London, 1961); Cobbett, *Rural Rides*, II, p. 241.
77. Armstrong, *Church, Methodists and Society*, pp. 130–5, 178–9; Davies and Rupp (eds.), *Methodist Church*, I, pp. 290–1.
78. Ward, *Religion and Society*, pp. 39–44; Gilbert, *Religion and Society*, pp. 73– 82; Best, *Temporal Pillars*, pp. 172– 84; Armstrong, *Church, Methodists and Society*, pp. 162–5; McClatchey, *Oxfordshire Clergy*, pp. 141–3, 146–50.
79. Henriques, *Religious Toleration*, pp. 15–17; Ward, *Religion and Society*, pp. 54–62; G. I. T. Machin, *The Catholic Question in English Politics, 1820–30* (Oxford, 1964), pp. 11–13.
80. G. M. Ditchfield, 'The Parliamentary Struggle over the Repeal of the Test and Corporation Acts, 1787–90', *English Historical Review*, LXXXIX (1974), pp. 551–77.
81. Thompson, *Working Class*, pp. 385–6, 430.
82. Halévy, *English People*, I, p. 485.
83. Machin, *Catholic Question*, pp. 12–15; Henriques, *Religious Toleration*, pp. 167–71; Halévy, *English People*, I, pp. 480–3.
84. Machin, *Catholic Question*, pp. 42–6; J. C. Beckett, *The Making of Modern Ireland, 1603–1923* (London, 1966), pp. 299–300.
85. Machin, *Catholic Question*, pp. 49–67.
86. J. H. Hexter, 'The Protestant Revival and the Catholic Question in England, 1778–1829', *Journal of Modern History*, VIII (1936), p. 303. See also Machin, *Catholic Question*, chs. 5–8; G. I. T. Machin, 'Resistance to the Repeal of the Test and Corporation Acts, 1828', *Historical Journal*, XXII (1979), pp. 115–39.
87. Machin, *Catholic Question*, pp. 168–9, 172–3.

88. G. F. A. Best, 'The Protestant Constitution and its Supporters, 1800–29', *Transactions of the Royal Historical Society*, 5th Series, VIII (1958), pp. 105–27.
89. O. J. Brose, *Church and Parliament: The Reshaping of the Church of England, 1828–60* (Stanford, 1959), pp. 9–10; E. Halévy, *History of the English People in the Nineteenth Century: III. The Triumph of Reform* (London, 1950), pp. 3–9, 41–3.
90. Brose, *Church and Parliament*, p. 21.
91. Brose, *Church and Parliament*, pp. 34–40, 58–97, 149, 198–204 (quotation from Blomfield, p. 36); Best, *Temporal Pillars*, pp. 270–9; G. F. A. Best, 'The Constitutional Revolution, 1828–32', *Theology*, LXII (1959), pp. 228–9, 231–4; Gilbert, *Religion and Society*, pp. 129–38; McClatchey, *Oxfordshire Clergy*, pp. 31, 90–3, 123–34.

THE PLATES

These notes are prefixed with the relevant number in the *Catalogue of Political and Personal Satires Preserved in the Department of Prints and Drawings in the British Museum* (eds. F. G. Stephens and M. D. George) 11 vols. 1870–1954, which should be consulted for further information. This is followed by the date of publication and engraver, where known.

1. BMC 10   (Temp. Eliz.?)
   A typical print on the martyrdoms of Mary's reign showing both the cruelty of Catholics and the way Catholic priests sought to dominate the laity.

2. BMC 13 (c.1627?) Danckertsz
Shows the traitorous plotting of Papists against Elizabeth, culminating in Gunpowder Plot, and so illustrates the belief that Papists were an alien 'fifth column', subjects of the pope rather than of the English crown.

POPISH PLOTS AND TREASONS

From the beginning of the Reign of Queen Elizabeth. Illustrated with Emblems and explain'd in Verse.

Figure 1.

The Pope slott on Armed Shoulders Rides,
And in vain Hopes the English spoils divides;
His Leaden bulls' vaunt grand Edicts roares,
And scatters the Rebellion round our shoars.
The Priest blesses the Villains, Cheats them on,
And promises Heav'ns Crown, when her Crown is won,
But God doth blast their Troops, their Councils mock,
And beings bold Traitors turth deserved block,

Figure 3.

Spains King, and Romes Triple-Crown'd Prelate joyn,
And with them both bold Stukely does Combine
Ireland to conquer. And the Pope has sent,
For that Black work, an Holy Regiment;
But in their way at Barbary they call,
Where at one blow the Moors destroy them All.
See here, what such Ambitious Traitors Gate,
The shame of Christians is by Pagans Slain,

Figure 5.

What truly Janizaries are Monks to Rome,
From their dark Cells the blackest Treasons come.
By the Popes Licenfe horrid Crimes they Act,
And Gold with piety each Treacherous Act.
A seminary Priest, like Comets Blaze,
Doth always Blood shed and Rebellion Raise;
But still the fatal Gibbet's ready first
For such, where Treason's with Religion mixt.

Figure 7.

Whilst Spains Embassador here Leiger lies,
Designs are laid the English to surprises,
Two Cataloguer is a Secretary had Got
The better two effect the Hellish Plot.
One all our Hatters Names, where Foes might Land,
T'other what Papists were to lend an hand,
For this base Trick he's forc'd to pack to Spain
Whilst Tyburn greets confederates that remain.

Figure 9.

The Jesuites vile Doctrines do Convince
Parry, Tis Merit for to kill his Prince,
The fatal Dagger he prepares with Art,
And means to sheath it in her Royal Heart,
Oft he Attempts, and is as oft put by,
By the Majestick Terrors of her Eye;
At last his Cursed Treasons be Confest
And So his welcom'd a fit Tyburn Guest;

Figure 11.

Nor was 't with Spain alone, Great Betty's Strife,
Now France attempts upon her precious Life;
The Guises castle th' Ambassador to bribe
Moody, and others, of the Roman Tribe,
To Cut her off. To which they Soon Consent,
But watchful Heav'n does that Guilt prevent,
Stafford cloth to the Councel All disclose,
And Home with shame perfidious Monsieur goes.

Figure 13.

But now a private horrid Treason view
Hatch't by the Pope, the Devil, and a Jew;
Lopez a Doctor must by Poyson do
What all their Plots have fail'd in hitherto;
What will you give me then, the Judas Cries,
Fifty thousand Crowns, t'other replies,
Tis done,— but hold, the wretch shall miss his hope,
The Treason known, and his Reward's the Rope.

Figure 15.

No Sooner James had blest the English Throne,
But Traiterous Priests Conspire to pull him down.
Watson the perfidious Maxime does Infuse,
And draws some Nobles to Join in the Ill,
But Princes then appear the most divine,
When they with unexpected Mercy Shine.
Just as the Fatal Ax attempts the Stroke,
Pardon stops in and does the Blow Revoke,

And now let us, with cheerful Hymns of praise,
And Hearts inflam'd with love an After tafte
Of Gratitude to God, who doth advance
Hi-out-firetch Arm to our Deliverance,
Tis only He, that doth protect his Sheep,
T'who alone doth this poor Island keep
From Romish Wolves, which would us from devour,
It not Defended by his mighty power,
Tis he that doth tour Church with fruitsome Comfort,
And beats that Popish superstition down,
Under her feet, and only they never rife,
Since Heaven whofe mercy ever are moft tender
Hath both refcu'd out Faith, and Faiths Defender.

Figure 2.

Don John, who under Spain did with proud Hand
The then unknown Netherlands Command,
Conceives for Englands Conqueft, and does Hope
To Gain it by Donation from the Pope,
Yet to frustr. our Queen does still pretend
Perpetual peace, and means will seem a friend;
But Heav'n looks through these juggles and in's prime,
Grief Cuts off Him and's Hopes All at a time,

Figure 4.

The Priests, with Crosses Ensigns-like displaid,
Prompt bloody Desmond to their spoiles be made
On Irish Protestants, and from afar
Blow Triumphs to Rebellions Holy War;
But sage'd Providence all Arts are vain,
The Crafty, in their Craft are over-ta'n;
Behold where falls the Stubborn Traitor lies,
Whilst to the Woods his Ghostly Father flies,

Figure 6.

Mad Summervil, by Cruel Priests infpird
To Do whatever mischeife they requir'd,
Sweats that he instantly will be the death
Of good and Gracious Queen Elizabeth,
Alas! is her Guards, but Heav'n protecting paw'r
Defeats his rage makes him a Prisoner:
Where to avoid a jest, though Shameful Death,
Self-Strangling hands do Stop his loathsome breath.

Figure 8.

View here a Miracle —— A Priest Convey,
In Spanish Bottom o're the path-less Seas,
Close treacherous Notes, whilst a Dutch Ship comes by
And freight Engag'd her well-known Enemy,
The Concealed Priest his Guilty Papers stain.
And over board the scattered fragments heart ;
But the just winds do force them back o'th' Decks,
And pciece-meal all the lurking plot detects.

Figure 10.

Here Babington and all his desperate Band,
Ready prepar'd for Royal Murder stand,
His Motto seems to glory in the Deed,
Theise my Companions are whose dangers lead,
Cowardly Traitors, so many Combine
To Cut off one poor Ladies vital Twine;
In vain,— Heaven is here Guard, and as for you 5
Behold, the Hangman gives you all your due,

Figure 12.

Spains proud armada whom the Pope did bless,
Arrogates ore the Confusion of Europe;
But Heav'n just Blast doth Scatter all their force,
They fly and quite round downward take their Courfes
So many takens, burnt, and Sunk th'ir Army,
Scarce one is Found to gee home News;
Thus England like Noahs Ark, amidst the Waves
Indulgent providence from Danger Saves,

Figure 14.

The Great Tyrone that did to often overaw
Ireland with Brood, and sweats their Romans,
Here vanquishit Swears, upon his bended knee,
To the Queens Deputy loyaltty,
Yet breaks that vow, and loaded with the Guilt
Of perjuries and Blood which he had foilt,
Being forc'd at last to fly his Native Land,
Carries in's Recall a Sting, a Scourge in's hand

Figure 16.

In this Curs'd Powder-plot we plainly see
The Quintessence of Romish Cruelty,
King Lords and Commons in one Hellish Blaft
Had been destroy'd, and all our Land laid waft,
No raze, within dark Lanthorn, ready stands
To Light the fatal Train with wicked hands,
But Heaven All-feeing eye defeats their deftin,
And faves us at a stand itiarcle from the fire ;

Let men both a just Adherence pay,
And for their prayer answers: joy.
Since this Traode happy done hath turned ore fore,
O may it never, never Leaves us more,

Sold by John Garret at his Shop, at the Exchange Staires in Cornhill where you may have choice of all Sorts of Large and Small Maps, Drawing Books Copy books, and Pictures for Gentlewomens works: and also very good originals of French and Dutch Prints.

IN NOMINE DOMINI *incepit Omne Malum*

A THANKFULL REMEMBRANCE OF GODS MERCIE

3. BMC 67   (c.1615)   R. Smith/M. Droshaut
   Note the references to Antichrist (usually identified as the pope at this time), the Gowrie conspiracy (against James I while king of Scotland) and the recent assassination of Henry IV of France.

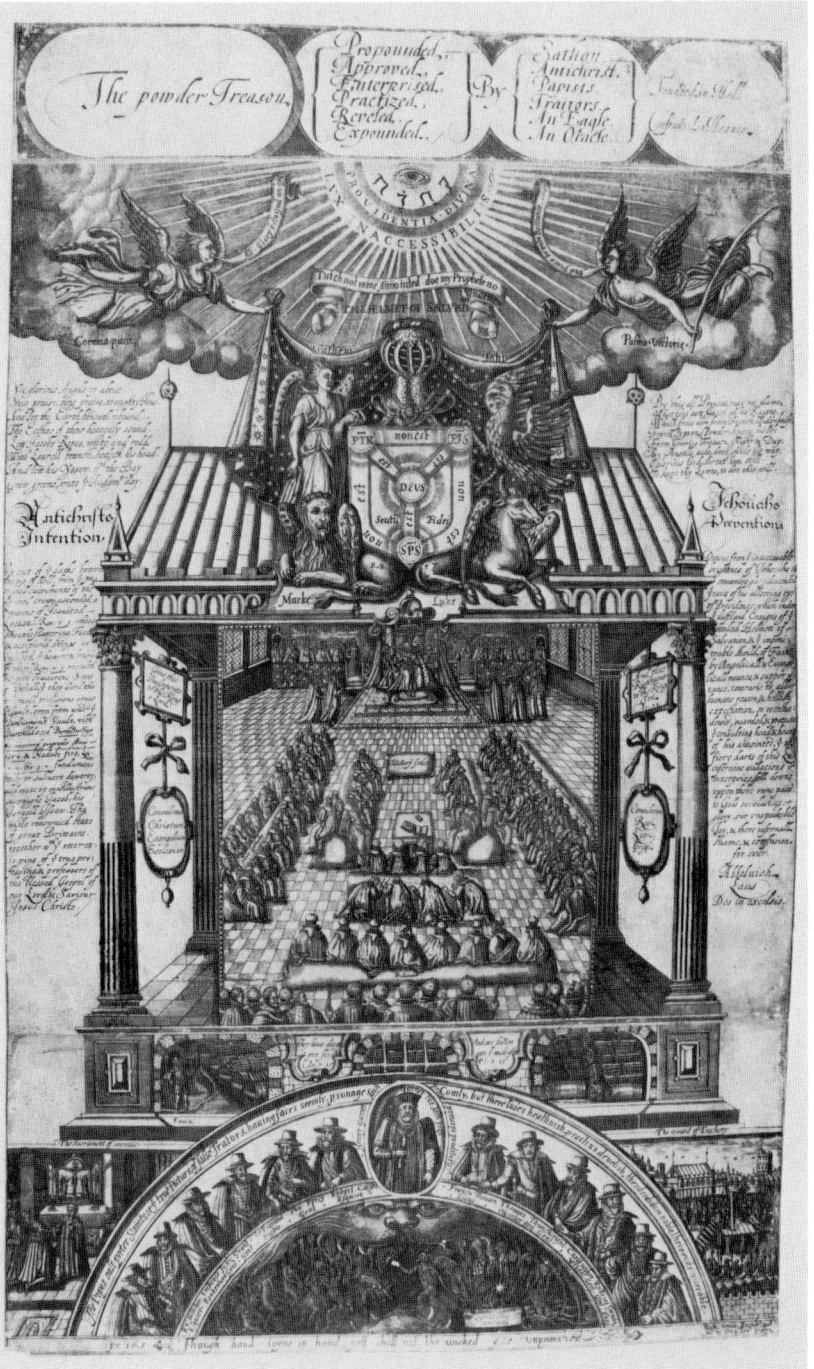

4. BMC 137   (c.1641)   W. Hollar
   Prynne (along with Burton and Bastwick – see BMC 138–9) was punished by the Court of Star Chamber for attacking bishops; both the bishops and their innovations were denounced as 'Popish'.

Mr: William Prynne, for writing a booke against Stage-players called Histrio-mastix was first censured in the Starr-Chamber to loose both his Eares in the pillorie, fined 5000ˡⁱ & perpetuall imprisonment in the Towre of London After this, on a meer suspition of writing other bookes, but nothing at all proved against him, hee was again censured in the Starr-chamber to loose the small remainder of both his eares in the pillorie, to be Stigmatized on both his Cheekes with a firey-iron, was fined again 5000ˡⁱ and banished into yᵉ Isle of Iersey, there to suffer perpetuall-close-imprisonmᵗ: no freinds being permitted to see him, on pain of imprisonment.

5. BMC 148 (c.1640) W. Hollar
   In May 1640 Convocation approved new canons (laws) for the Church, including the oath not to alter its government by archbishops, bishops, 'etc.' (which some took to mean the pope). In December the Commons declared these canons illegal.

This Canons seal'd, well forg'd, not made of lead
Give fire. O noe 't will breake and strike vs dead.

That I.A.B. doe sweare that I doe approve the Doctrine and Discipline or Government established in the Church of England, as containing all things necessary to Salvation; And that I will not endeavour by my selfe or any other, directly or indirectly to bring in any Popish Doctrine, contrary to that which is so established. Nor will I ever give my consent to alter the Government of this Church by Archbishops, Bishops, Deanes, and Arch-Deacons, &c as it stands now established, and as by right it ought to stand: Nor yet ever to subject it to the usurpations and superstitions of the Sea of Rome. And all these things I doe plainly and sincerely acknowledge and sweare, according to the plain and common sence, and understanding of the same words, without any equivocation or mentall evasion, or secret reservation whatsoever. And this I doe heartily, willingly and truly, upon the faith of a Christian: So help me God in Iesus Christ.

Prime, lay the Trayne, thus you must mount, and levell,
    then shall we gett the day. *but freind the Devill.*
Turne, wheele about, take tyme, and stand your ground,
    this Canon cannot faile, *but tis not sound.*
Feare not, weel cast it, 'tis a desperate case,
    weel sweare it, and enjoyne it, *but tis base.*
The Mettalls brittle, and tis ram'd so hard,
    with an *Oath* &c: that hath fowly marr'd
All our designes, that now we have no hope
    but in the service of *our Lord the Pope.*
Dissolve the Rout, each man vnto his calling
    which had we kept, we had not now beene falling

6. BMC 220   Dec. 1641
   Shows the difference of emphasis between Laudians and Puritans. The former stressed the liturgy, as set out in the Prayer Book, the latter the pre-eminence of the sermon. In order to safeguard their sermons, the citizens are ready to abolish bishops. Note the pope riding the Beast (of Revelation).

THE BISHOPS LAST GOOD-NIGHT.

Where Popery and Innovations doe begin,   There Treason will by degrees come in.

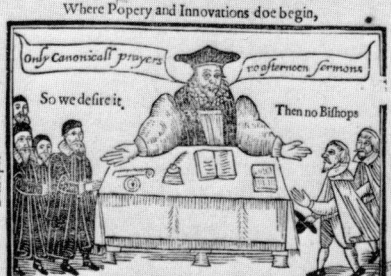

If they had ruld still, where had we been?   God keepe us from Prelates, Popish Prelates.

I.
COme downe Prelates, all arow,
Your Protestation brings you low,
Have not we alwayes told you so;
You are too sawcy Prelates,
Come downe Prelates.

II.
Canterbury your Armes from the Steeple high,
The stormes have caused low to lie,
You know not how soone your selfe may die,
Prepare your selfe *Canterbury*;
Downe must *Canterbury*.

III.
Yorke, when you were *Lincolne* of late,
You were in the *Tower*, yet still you will prate,
How dare you Protest against the whole State,
You are too bold *Yorke*,
Come downe proud *Yorke*.

IV.
Durham, how dare you be so bold,
To have the Parliament by you contrould,
T'were better you to the *Scots* had been sold,
You are deceived *Durham*,
Come downe old *Durham*.

V.
Coventry, and *Lichfeild*, your Popery is knowne,
T'were better you had let the Parliament alone,
But now it's too late to make your moane,
You are fast *Coventry*,
Come downe *Coventry*.

VI.
Norwich, is your Remonstrance come to this,
We now see what your humilitie is;
Were you removed from *Exeter* for this,
You are led away *Norwich*,
Come downe *Norwich*.

VII.
Asaph, what a change is here,
You that even now was so great a Peere,
And now a Prisoner this new yeare;
You must lie by it *Asaph*,
In the Tower *Asaph*.

VIII.
Bath and Wels, where is now thy hope,
Canst thou not get a pardon from the Pope,
To passe away without a Rope?
Where art thou *Bath and Wels?*
Down must *Bath and Wels*.

IX.
Hereford, was never so promoted,
Since out of the Convocation he was rooted,
To hasten this project it was well footed,
To bring thee down *Hereford*,
Down must *Hereford*.

X.
Oxford, the Students will curse thy fact,
For doing of such an ungodly Act,
Thy credit now is utterly crackt:
You are not for *Oxford*,
But the Tower *Oxford*.

XI.
Ely, thou hast alway to thy power,
Left the Church naked in a storme and showre,
And now (for't) thou must to thy old friend ith'
To the Tower must *Ely*,   (Tower;
Come away *Ely*.

XII.
Gloster, go tell old *William* now,
That thou art made perforce to bow,
Meerly drawn in, thou knowst though how,
You must away *Gloster*,
To prison poore *Gloster*.

XIII.
Peterborough, *England* knowes thee well,
Where is thy candle, book, and Bell?
Thy Pardons now will never sell,
There's no help *Peterborough*,
Go must *Peterborough*.

XIIII.
Landaff, provide for St. *Davids* day,
Left the Leeke, and Red-herring run away,
Are you resolved to go or to stay?
You are called for *Landaff*,
Come in *Landaff*.

FINIS.

London Printed in the yeer that ended,
When the Prelates Protestation against the *Parliament* was vended,
And they were sent to the Tower, as the old yeer ended,
By a dozen together,
In frosty weather.

Anno Dom. 1641.

7. BMC 319 (May 1642)
Again the bishops are identified with Popery. The term 'roundhead' is here used of a monk, perhaps in riposte to its use against Puritans.

{ See heer, Malignants Folterie } { The Sound-Head, Round-Head, Rattle-Head }
{ Retorted on them properly } { Well plac'd, where best is merited. }

Sound-Head   **Rattle-Head**   **Round-Head**

This Faithlesse World is full of foule mistakes,
Calls Virtue, Vice; & Goodnes, Badnes makes:
The Orthodox, Sound & Religious Man,
Atheist's call Round-Head here, a Puritan.
Because Hee, roundly Rattle-Heads, Truths foes,
Plainly depaints. If this next figure showes

See, heer, the Rattle-Heads most Rotten-Heart,
Acting the Atheists or Arminians part;
Vnder One Cater-cap a Ianus-face,
Repeating Truth, a Crucifixe t'embrace:
Thus Linsey Wolsie, Priestly Prelates vile,
With Romish rubbysh did mens Soules beguile

But heer's a Round Head to the purpose showne,
A Romish-Rounded Shaveling, too well knowne;
A Balld-pate Fryer, a Round-Head indeed,
Which doth (almost) Rotunditie exceed:
Since The Round-Heads, with Rattle-Heads so gree,
Romish Malignants: Round-Heads (right) may be.

8. BMC 377 (1643) W. Hollar
   Note especially articles 1 and 2, which helped determine the direction of church reform in the 1640s.

A Solemn LEAGUE AND COVENANT,

for Reformation, and defence of Religion, the Honour and happinesse of the king, and the Peace and Safety of the three Kingdoms of ENGLAND, SCOTLAND, and IRELAND.

We Noblemen, Barons, knights, Gentlemen, Citizens, Burgesses, Ministers of the Gospel, and Commons of all sorts in the Kingdomes of England, Scotland, and Ireland, by the Providence of God living under one king, and being of one reformed Religion, having before our eies the Glory of God, and the advancement of the kingdome of our Lord and Saviour Iesus Christ, the Honour and happinesse of the kings Maiesty and his posterity, and the true publique Liberty, Safety, and Peace of the Kingdomes, wherein every ones private Condition is included: and calling to minde the treacherous and bloody Plots, Conspiracies, Attempts, and Practices of the Enemies of God, against the true Religion, and professors thereof in all places, especially in these three kingdomes ever since the Reformation of Religion, and how much their rage, power and presumption, are of late, and at this time increased and exercised, whereof the deplorable state of the Church and kingdom of Ireland, the distressed estate of the Church and Kingdom of England, and the dangerous estate of the Church and kingdom of Scotland, are present and publique Testimonies. We have now at last, after other meanes of Supplication, Remonstrance, Protestations and Sufferings, for the preservation of our selves and our Religion, from utter Ruine and Destruction, according to the commendable practice of these kingdomes in former times, and the Example of Gods people in other Nations, after mature deliberation, resolved and determined to enter into a mutuall and solemn League and Covenant, Wherein we all subscribe, and each one of us for himself, with our hands lifted up to the most high God, do sweare,

I. That we shall sincerely, really and constantly, through the Grace of God, endeavour in our severall places and callings, the preservation of the Reformed Religion in the Church of Scotland, in Doctrine, Worship, Discipline & Government against our common Enemies, the reformation of Religion in the kingdomes of England and Ireland in Doctrine, Worship, Discipline and Government, according to the Word of God, and the Example of the best Reformed Churches, And shall endeavour to bring the Churches of God in the three kingdoms to the neerest coniunction and Uniformity in Religion, Confession of Faith, Form of Church government, Directory for Worship and Catechising: That we and our posterity after us may, as Brethren live in Faith and Love, and the Lord may delight to dwell in the midest of us.

II. That we shall in like manner, without respect of persons, indeavour the extirpation of Popery, Prelacie, (that is Church government, by Arch Bishops, Bishops, their Chancellors and Comissaries, Deans, Deans and Chapters, Archdeacons, & all other Ecclesiasticall Officers depending on that Hierarchy) Superstition, Heresie, Schisme, Prophanenesse, and whatsoever shall be found to be contrary to sound Doctrine, and the power of Godlinesse: lest we partake in other mens sins, and therby be in danger to receive of their plagues, and that the Lord may be one, and his Name one in the three kingdoms.

III. We shall with the same sincerity, reality and constancy, in our severall Vocations, endeavour with our estates and lives, mutually to preserve the Rights and Priviledges of the Parliaments, and the Liberties of the Kingdomes, and to preserve and defend the Kings Maiesties person and authority, in the preservation and defence of the true Religion, and Liberties of the kingdomes, that the World may beare witnesse with our consciences of our Loyaltie, and that we have no thoughts or intentions to diminish his Maiesties iust power and greatnesse.

IV. We shall also with all faithfulnesse endeavour the discovery of all such as have beene, or shall be Incendiaries, Malignants, or evill Instruments, by hindering the Reformation of Religion, dividing the King from his people or one of the kingdomes from another, or making any faction or parties amongst the people contrary to this league & Covenant, that they may be brought to publick triall, and receive condigne punishment, as the degree of their offences shall require or deserve, or the supreame Iudicatories of both kingdoms respectively, or others having power from them for that effect, shall judge convenient.

A Malignant

A Preist

V. And whereas the happinesse of a blessed Peace between these kingdoms, denyed in former times to our Progenitors, is by the good Providence of God granted unto us, and hath been lately concluded and setled by both Parliaments, we shall each one of us, according to our place and interest, indeavour that they may remain conioyned in a firm Peace an Union to all posterity: And that Iustice may be done upon the wilfull Opposers thereof, in manner expressed in the precedent Article.

A threefold cord is not easily broken

England Scotland Ireland

VI. We shall also according to our places & callings in this common cause of Religion, Liberty and Peace of the Kingdomes, assist and defend all those that enter into this League and Covenant, in the maintaining & pursuing thereof, and shall not suffer our selves directly or indirectly by whatsoever combination, perswasion or terror to be devided & withdrawn from this blessed Union & coniungtion, whether to make defection to the contrary part, or to give our selves to a detestable indifferency or neutrality in this cause which so much concerneth the glory of God, the good of the kingdoms, and honour of the king, but shall all the dayes of our lives zealously and constantly continue therein against all opposition, and promote the same according to our power, against all Lets and impediments whatsoever, and what we are not able our selves to suppresse or overcome, we shall reveale and make known, that it may be timely prevented or removed: All which we shall do as in the sight of God.

And because these kingdoms are guilty of many sins & provocations against God, & his Son Iesus Christ, as is too manifest by our present distresses and dangers the fruits thereof. We professe and declare before God and the world our unfained desire to be humbled for our, & for the sins of these kingdoms, especially that we have not as we ought, valued the inestimable benefit of the Gospel that we have not laboured for the purity and power thereof, and that we have not endeavored to receive Christ in our hearts, nor to walk worthy of him in our lives, which are the causes of other sinns and transgressions so much abounding amongst us: And our true and unfained purpose, desire and endeavour for our selves, and all others under our power and charge both in publick, and in private, in all duties we owe to God, and man, to amend our lives and each one to go before another in the Example of a reall Reformation, that the Lord may turne away his wrath, and heavy indignation, and establish these Churches and kingdoms in truth and peace. And this Covenant we make in the presence of Almighty God, the Searcher of all hearts, with a true intention to performe the same as we shall answer at that great day when the secrets of all hearts shall be disclosed. Most humbly beseeching the Lord to strengthen us by his Holy Spirit to this end, and to blesse our endeavours and proceedings with such successe, as may be deliverance and safety to his people, & encouragement to other Christian Churches groaning under, or in danger of the yoake of Antichristian Tyranny to yoyne in the same or the like Association and Covenant, to the glory of God, the enlargement of the kingdome of Iesus Christ, and the peace and tranquility of Christian kingdomes & Commonwealths.

9. BMC 380   (July 1643)   J. Ward
   This reflects the hopes of the early 1640s of godly reform and of a purer church built on the ruins of that of Laud.

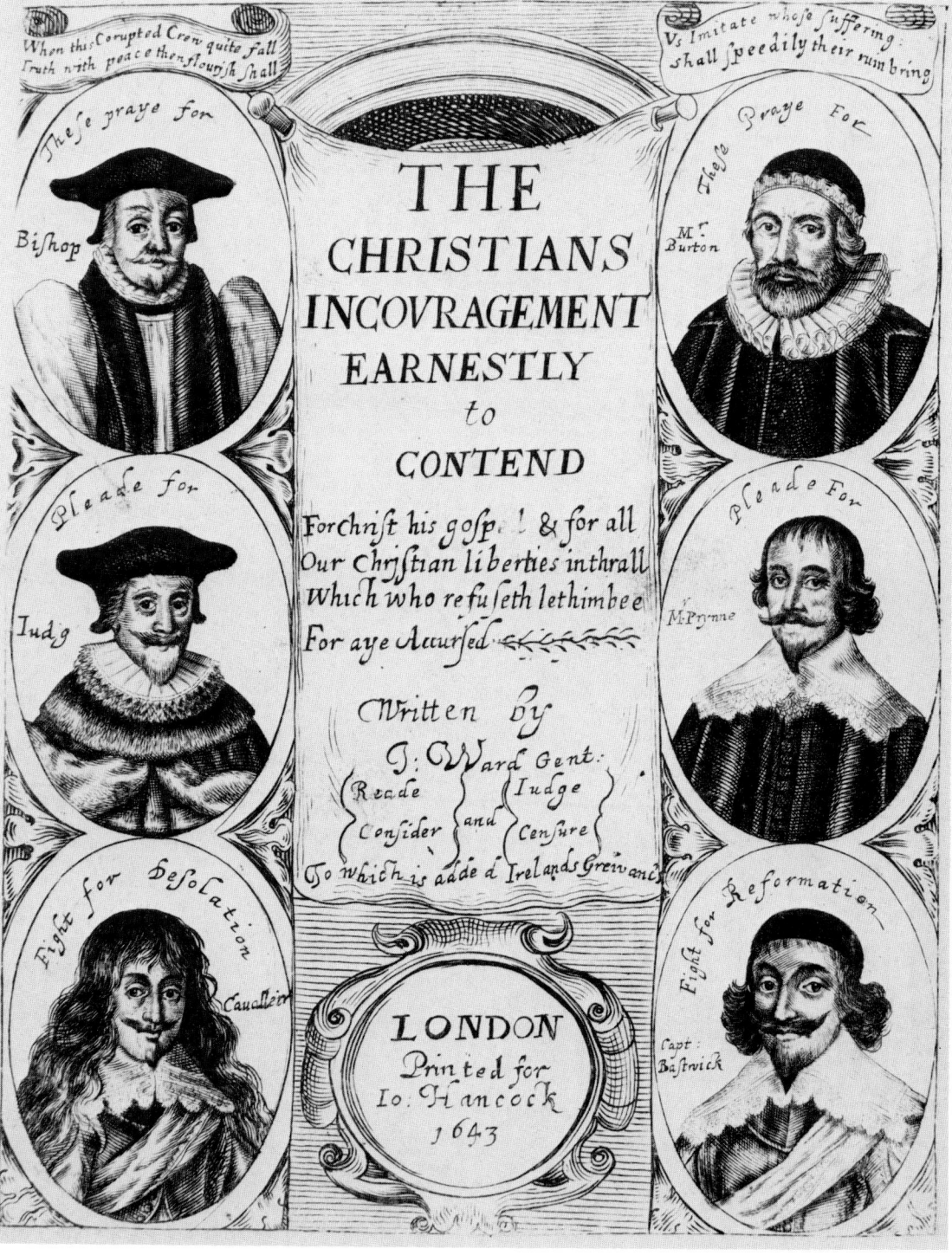

10. BMC 166 (1644) W. Hollar
The trial of Archbishop Laud. Note the presence of Prynne, Burton and Bastwick.

PROVERBS 11. 8.

The Righteous is delivered out of Trouble, and the wicked commeth in his stead.

A. The Arch-Bishop of *Canterbury*.
B. The Gentleman Usher with his Black-Rod.
C. The Leiutenant of the Tower. D. The Bishops Courcell.
E. The Clarke that reades the Evidence.
F. The Table where the Books and Papers given in evidence lay.
G. The Members of the House of Commons, and Mr. *Prynne* standing in the midst of them, H. Mr. *Henry Burton*.
I. I. I. The witnesses, Mistris *Bastwicke*. Mr. *Baker* the Messenger.
K. K. K. The People and Auditors, within and without the Barre.
L. L. The LORDS. M. M. The Judges and Assistants.
N. The Speaker of the Lords House. T. The Hangings of 88. S. Mich. S▫

11. BMC 412 (1645)
After his trial, Laud vomits out the canons, etc., which have brought him to his present extremity.

12. BMC 247   (1645?)
    This shows the separatists as 'the canker worms' of Protestantism (Edwards used the term *Gangraena*) and alleges that they work with the Catholics. It stresses the need for order and for mixing saints and sinners within a congregation: churches were not for the elect alone.

A
Whip for the back of a backsliding
BROVVNIST.

Helpe Neighbours helpe, good women come with speed,
For of your helpe there never was more neede,
Mid-wives make haste and dresse you as you run,
Either come quickly or we're all undone,
The words in labour, her throwes comes so quick,
That with her paine shee's growne starke lunatick,
For I did aske one of her Bratts of late:
Why the Lords Prayer was almost out of date,
He told me Christ had new Disciples now,
That of set forme of Prayer would not allow;
Alasse said I are they so dainty growne,
Such a fantastick Crew was never knowne,
These are the Bretheren of the Seperation,
The Cancer wormes of this our English Nation,
And it is feard if they be let alone,
These wormes will knaw the Kingdome to the Bone
These with the Papists breed the mischeife here,
Whilst Cockle Branes builds Castles in the aire,
Who Parrot like they having learnd to prate,
Disturbe the Church the Common-wealth and State,
Yea Church disturbers learnings Enemyes,
Yea seeming Saints, yea painted Butter flyes,
Yea Bug-beares of a Kingdom silly Elues,
Whose Zeale transporte you quite beyond your ielues,
Oh know you what you doe, that yea presist,
Still day by day in doing what you list,
Shame to our Kingdome if this suffer'd bee,
From hombre I trowe we never shall be free,
If that you rule the rost you Moone-Calues all,
Why doe you force my Muse to reiling fall,
That never was accustomed to scould,
Had not so good a Cause made me so bold.

Gods sperit evermore good sperits makes,
Then if your sperits of Gods sperits pertakes,
You will be ruld by order, not by will,
God is the same, the God of order still:

And you cannot be his Disciples right,
That end what you begin in hate and spight,
I judge no man but what their actions show
Brings me of force to judge of what I know,
Good Sister Mag-pye and good Brother Daw,
That leapes o're hills and stumbells at a straw:
I pray be patient trouble not the State,
Your friends at Amsterdam do for you waite,
Mistake me not I speake but this to prove you,
I de rather have you stay because I love you,
Yet if you stay I'de have you know what's ment,
Betwixt an Idol and an Ornament,
Which if you doe I should be glad to heare,
That to our Church once more you would repare,
Which though it be of Stone should not be hated,
Cause to GODS service it is consecrated,
I know nor what your Barnes and Stables were,
Where Asses bray, pray understand and heare,
I speake unfainedly I blush to see,
Such men so wise in show such Fooles to bee,
What though the good and bad together meer,
Within the Church as well as in the Street,
Shall we refraine the Church ever the more,
Alasse alasse your Argument is poore:
How angry were the Pharisees and why,
Because our Saviour Christ kept Company
With Publicans and Sinners thinke on this,
And rectifie your judgements that s amisse.

You being good shall in the Chansell sit,
The wicked in the Bellfree as 'tis fit,
If they be so contented on Condition,
You'le come to Church and not run to perdition,
No Drunkard nor no Swearer shall sit neere you,
For to anoy or other wise to feare you,
Because I know you timerous are by nature,
And wonderous fearfull of a wicked Creature,
The Booke of Common Prayer refind shall bee,
Or you shall pray extempory, and be free
From all occasion of a thing so common,
No not so much as looke upon a woman:
They shall sit by themselves, let this suffice
For feare your sperits on a suddaine rise,
And leaue away your mindes from what is good,
Brethren we know you are but flesh and blood.

Vpon Condition you to Church will go,
I'le doe the best I can to have it so,
Which if I do I hope I am your Friend,
As I desire to be, and so I end.   Finis.

LONDON, Printed for Humphrey Chrouch.

13. BMC 385   (1645?)
    Adoniram Byfield was a member of the Westminster Assembly of Divines and one of the compilers of the Directory.

14. BMC 419   (Feb. 1645)
    Frontispiece to Daniel Featley, *The Dippers Dipt*. Believers in adult baptism found it difficult to shake off their reputation for extremism, violence and sexual licence, which derived from the Anabaptist regime in Münster in the 1530s.

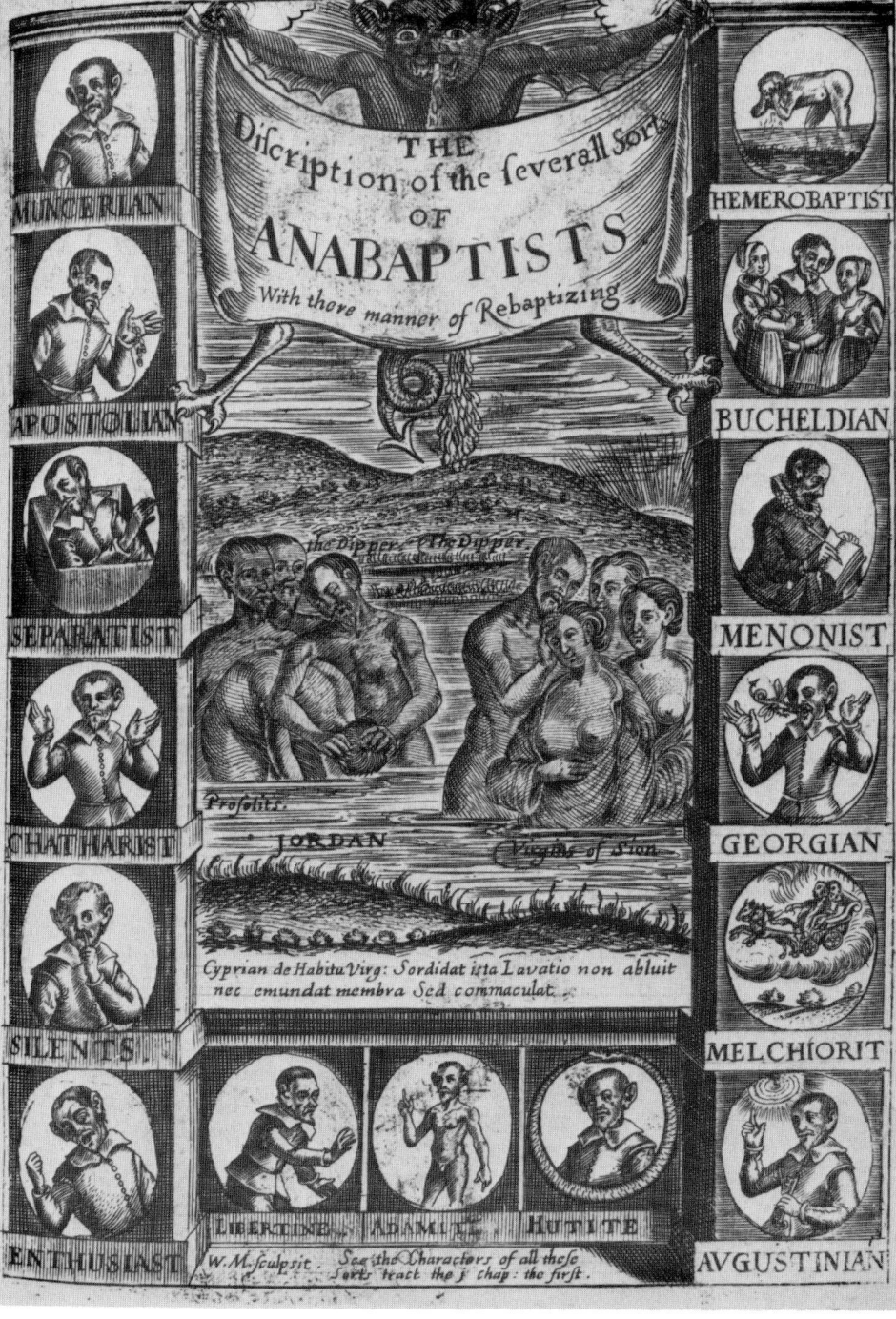

15. BMC 426   (Nov. 1645)   W. Marshall
Frontispiece to F. Quarles *The Shepherds Oracles*. A rare episcopalian print, showing Charles I and his bishops trying to protect true religion against the assaults of Jesuits and tub preachers (with the implication that these are working together).

16. BMC 666   Jan. 1647
    A Presbyterian attack on the eccentricities which could result from separatism.
    See also BMC 819.

A Catalogue of the severall Sects and Opinions in England and other Nations.
With a briefe Rehearsall of their false and dangerous Tenents.

Labels on figures (top row): Jesuit | [Welsh-man saying hee was Christ] | Arminian | Arian | Adamite | Libertin
(bottom row): Ante-Scripturian | Soule-Sleeper | Anabaptist | Familist | Seeker | Divorcer

Jesuit.
By hellish wiles the States to ruine bring,
My Tenents are to murder Prince or King:
If I obtaine my projects, or seduce,
Then from my Treasons I will let them loose:
And since the Roman Papall State doth totter,
I'le frame my sly-conceits to worke the better.

Socinian.
By cunning art my way's more neatly spun,
Although destructive to profession;
Obscuring truths, although substantiall,
To puzle Christians or to make them fall:
That precious time may not be well improv'd,
Ile multiply strange notions for the lewd.

Arminian.
Would any comfortlesse both live and die?
Let him learne free wills great uncertaintie:
Salvation that doth unmov'd remaine,
Arminian Logick would most maintaine,
And faith that's founded on a firme decree,
Is plac't by them to cause uncertaintie.

Arrian.
What they dare to deny, Christians know, (flow,
Christ God and Man, from whom their comforts
'Tis sad, that Christians dive by speculation,
Whereby they loose more sweeter contemplation:
Where Christian practice acts the life of grace,
There's sweet content to run in such a race.

Adamite.
Hath Adams sin procur'd his naked shame,
With leaves at first that thought to hide his staine?
Then let not Adamites in secret dare
Aparent sinfull acts to spread; but feare,
Since Adams sin hath so defil'd poore dust,
Cast from this Paradise by wicked lust.

Libertine.
A pish at sin and open violation,
By wilfull lust, deserves just condemnation:
Repentance, though a Riddle, this he say,
Thou must unfold the same or perish aye.
Then least this holy Law thou see dost slight,
Shall presse thee one day with a dreadfull weight.

Antiscripturian.
By cursed words and actions to gainsay
All Scripture-truth, that ought to guide thy way,
Without all question, were it in thy power,
Thou would'st all sacred Rules at once devoure:
Poore man, forbeare, thou strov'st but all in vaine,
Since all mans might shall but confirme the same.

Soule-sleeper.
That soules are mortall, some have di'd to say,
And by their lives, this folly some bewray;

Whilst (like the beast) they only live to eat,
In sinfull pleasures wast their time and state:
Meantime forgetting immortality,
To woe or joy for all eternity.

Anabaptist.
Poore men contrive strange fancies in the braine,
To cleanse that guilt which is a Leopard staine:
'Tis but a fain'd conceit, contended for,
Since water can but act its outward matter:
Regenerate, new-born, these babes indeed
Of watry Elements have little need.

Familist.
Were all things Gospell that H.N. hath said,
A strange confused worke were newly laid:
A perfect state, like Adams, is pretended,
Whilst outwardly each day God is offended:
No Sabboth, but alike all daies shall be,
If Familists may have their Liberty.

Seeker.
All Ordinances, Church and Ministry,
The Seeker that hath lost his beaten way,
Denies: for miracles he now doth waite,
Thus glorious truths reveal'd are out of date:
Is it not sad such men should alwaies doubt
Of clearest truths, in Holy Writ held out.

Divorcer.
To warrant this great Law of Separation,
And make one two, requires high aggravation:
Adultery onely cuts the Marriage-knot,
Without the which Gods Law allowes it not.
Then learne to seperate from sin that's common,
And man shall have more Comfort from a woman.

Pelagian.
What Adams state had been without a fall,
Is but presumption to contend withall:
But Adams state of deprivation
Profits by serious meditation;
Men it keep backe, Christ's all in all to all,
Then live by faith obedientiall.

Separatist or Independant.
The Saints Communion Christians do professe,
Most necessary to the life of grace,
But whilst some throwd them by this bare notion,
Condemning all the rest for Antichristian,
Preserving much confused sad distraction,
Tacy thus disturb a settlement i'th' Nation,

Antinomians.
Under this name shrowds many desperate
Destroying Doctrines, unregenerate,
Espec: it opposing grace in its true power,
And glories laboriously do much shower:

Repentance and obedience are condemn'd,
And rarest Christian duties much contemn'd.

Anti-Sabbatarian.
This curst opinion long hath been on foot,
A Christian Sabboth from our file to root:
When for base pleasures or curst recreation,
On Lords daies duties lost by prophanation.
Divine example hints sufficiently,
A first daies Sabboths full Authority.

Anti-Trinitarians.
That dare to search into the Trinity,
And in divine distinctions much to pry:
Christs humane nature they would dare to staine,
As ours by Adams guilt, but all in vaine:
Then let's beware, least diving thus too far,
We leese our love, and much increase sad jar.

Apostolicks.
That now expect a new revealed way,
Unknowne in Scripture, they have dar'd to say,
Beyond the way of usuall dispensation
Guifts infallible with Revelation,
And miracles againe with Ministry,
Thus men are lost, when they too far do pry.

Thraskites.
The Jewish Sabboth these would have remaine,
As warrantable by command most plaine:
But since the Priest and sacrifice are ceast,
That Sabboth Judaicall is decreast:
The Lords daies ravishment divinely is
Confirm'd by Practice which unerring is.

Hetheringtonians.
That Englands Church is false do firmely hold,
What truths are therein taught deny this bold
Without true ground, there's many yet that say
As much as these that erre and go astray:
Oh could we keep within a Christian bound,
That should sad sad division not be found.

The Tatians.
In what time that Eusebius lived, have
All Pauls Epistles dar'd reject and have
The Acts of the Apostles set at nought,
Thus strange opinions have confusion brought:
Not far from those are some now in our daies,
That leave the Word and act contrary waies.

The Marchionites.
All Matthew, Marke, and Johns divine
Most sacred Writ, these Gospels trine,
Tertullian doth report, rejected were,
By this strange Sect, thus heretofore:
As now we see, division greatly spread,
And from the bounds of practice get a head.

WE read how that in the last daies many false Prophets shall arise, and many shall say, Loe here is Christ, loe there is Christ, and shall deceive many, 2 Pet. 2. 1. there were false Prophets also among the people, as there shall bee false teachers among you, who privily shall bring in damnable heresies, even denying the Lord that bought them, and bring upon themselves swift destruction, therefore we had need to be established in the truth, as in 1 Cor. 16. 13. stand fast in the faith, 1 Pet. 5. 9. whom resist stedfast in the faith, 1 Joh. 2. 23. Let that therefore abide in you which yee have heard from the beginning, and yee shall continue in the Sonne and in the Father, Vers. 25. These things I have written unto you, concerning them that seduce you. Many strange Sects and Opinions are held amongst us, so that it is to be feared, that what rule soever our wise and honourable Parliament shall establish, it will not content the unquiet spirits of a lawlesse generation, which would have no rule; for set any Rule in the Church they will call it persecution, and they say they dislike some things commanded because they are imposed. Some there are that looke for a Temporall Kingdome of Christ, that shall last a thousand years; this opinion is most dangerous for all States, for they teach that all the ungodly must be killed, and that the wicked have no propriety in their estates; Others out of confidence that they are ruled by the spirit, despise all ordinary calling to the Ministry, all written prayers, all helps of study: Some make no conscience to heare and bring Psalms, but rather follow their own inventions, as he that would not believe the sun because it went not with his watch: Likewise this ordinary saying of theirs; Be in Christ and sin if thou canst; meaning, that regenerate men cannot sinne; this is the Doctrine of the Anabaptists: also that to receive the Communion with a prophane person, is to partake of his sinne; that the Lords Prayer was never taught to be said; that the Gospell was never purely taught since the Apostles times; that a liberty of Prophecying must be allowed; that all humane Lawes must be abolished; that Ministers of Gods Word should rule both the Spirituall and the Temporall; that abstraction of Parishes is Antichristian. Should these absurd and grosse opinions take place, what division and confusion would they work amongst us? but such is the wisdome and care of our worthy and pious Parliament, to provide an Ordinance for preventing of the growing and spreading of heretic

Jan: 19th Printed by R.A. 1647, 1646

17. BMC 670   Feb. 1647
Another Presbyterian print, arguing that despite their cries of persecution, the Independents are the real persecutors as they revile godly ministers and the Westminster Assembly.

The Picture of an English Persecutor or a Foole Ridden Ante-Presbeterian Sectary

For opposeing Authority Reuileing the Assembly
Slandering the Gouernment by Presbetry and
disturbing the ministers at the time of their publique
excercise by giueing up bills in mockery calling the
ministers preists rideing slaues, horse leeches Cormorants
gorbelly'd Idoll Consistory of deuills etc: hath not this dis=
couer'd Ishmaels carnall spirits persecuting godly Isaaks

18. BMC 675   March 1647
   An unusual print urging Presbyterians and Independents to join against the common enemy, the Papists.

19. BMC 680   May 1647
Frontispiece to *The Discovery of Witches* by Matthew Hopkins, the notorious 'witchfinder general'. Since about 1620 there had been few convictions for witchcraft but Hopkins' activities brought about a brief, but intense upsurge of prosecutions. How far his motives were religious or financial remains open to question.

20. BMC 766   Dec. 1649
   An Independent or sectarian piece, equating 'new presbyter' with 'old priest' and denouncing all national churches as Antichristian. See also BMC 647.

AN EMBLEM OF ANTICHRIST

In his three fould Hirerchyes of Papacy, Prelacy, & Presbytery

As allso a description of the Trenatie in Vnitie, & Vnitie in Trenatie. (of their Lord God the Pope) in his Holyneses Dietie. 2.thes.2.4

Small Rome left for the Pope etc.

Prellat

Wee are all intirest Before ken to peeces

Pope

Let vs rent our church & Calling assunder

Presbiter

Oh Worship for it is God

1. Kings .18. 27. And it came to pass at Noone that Elijah mocked them saying &c.

I neede not put a Beareskin on A Beare Or pin a Devill to A Cauileare.

Rev: 16. 19. 20. 21.

And the Great City was devided into THREE PARTS etc.

21. BMC 777   Jan. 1650
   Typical denunciation of the Ranters, stressing their violence and rejection of the Bible's authority.

Bloudy Newſe from the North,
AND
The Ranting *Adamites* Declaration concerning the King of *Scotland*, with their new League, Covenant, and Proteſtation; their denying the great God of Heaven, and burning his ſacred word and Bible; the name of a new God by them choſen, and his Speech and promiſe unto them; their new Law, and grand Court; their Arraignment and Tryal, and a Copy of the ſeveral Articles and Indictment; with the ſeveral ſentences to be inflicted upon divers offenders, together with their names. Alſo, a bloudy Plot diſcovered, concerning their Reſolution to murther all thoſe that will not turn *Ranters*; put in execution at *York*, to the aſtoniſhment and admiration of the Reader, that ſhall diligently peruſe this inſuing Subject, never before heard of.

Jan: 20 Publiſhed according to Order. 1650

LONDON, Printed by J. C. 1650.

22. BMC 778   Nov. 1651
Similar to *21*, but with the main emphasis on promiscuity. Although the Ranters' heyday was brief, a few local groups survived into the eighteenth century: Waddy, *Bitter Sacred Cup*, p. 24; Thompson, *Working Class*, p. 39.

The Ranters Ranting:

WITH

The apprehending, examinations, and confession of *Iohn Collins*, *I. Shakespear*, *Tho. Wiberton*, and five more which are to answer the next Sessions. And severall songs or catches, which were sung at their meetings. Also their several kinds of mirth, and dancing. Their blasphemous opinions. Their belief concerning heaven and hell. And the reason why one of the same opinion cut off the heads of his own mother and brother. Set forth for the further discovery of this ungodly crew.

LONDON
Printed by B. Alsop, 1650.

23. BMC 158 (c.1653?)
Denounces both the Quakers' arrogance in seeking guidance from their 'inner light' rather than the Bible, and their alleged sexual immorality.

A QVAKER

Weake as you say we are, yett wee commandy,
all flesh to fall, that doth against us stand.
The light within us, of such force, is fownd,
showld satan come, twill lay him on the grvnd.

The Light they talke of keepes a heavy tout,
ile search all corners, but ile find it out.
By yea and nay, she is a dareing Gule,
ile try a fill, or els fam a Churle.

With face of brass, this woman that you see
most Impudently doth afirm, that shee
The mind of God, in all poynts, more doth know,
then from the Sacred Scriptures, ere could flow.
Presumptious wretch; it were more fitt that shee,
at home showld keepe, and mind hir howsewifery.
And if noe meanes to live on, woorke for bread,
then idlye gossop with hir maget head.

Their light within doth so prevayle,
it makes them hot about the tayle.
Exsept a freind that poynt doth cleare,
they could them selves in peeces teare.

24. BMC 885   April 1655
This attacks the Quakers' penchant for hysteria, their strange doctrines and alleged promiscuity. See also BMC 887.

THE QVAKERS DREAM:

OR,
The Devil's Pilgrimage in England:
BEING
An infallible Relation of their several Meetings,

Shreekings, Shakings, Quakings, Roarings, Yellings, Howlings, Tremblings in the Bodies, and Risings in the Bellies: With a Narrative of their several Arguments, Tenets, Principles, and strange Doctrine: The strange and wonderful Satanical Apparitions, and the appearing of the Devil unto them in the likeness of a black Boar, a Dog with flaming eyes, and a black man without a head, causing the Dogs to bark, the Swine to cry, and the Cattel to run, to the great admiration of all that shall read the same.

London, Printed for G. Horton, and are to be sold at the Royal Exchange in Cornhil, 1655.

25. BMC 746   (1649)

A later, unsigned copy of William Marshall's much-copied frontispiece to *Eikon Basilike* which was said to be a collection of Charles I's writings in prison. See F. F. Madan, *A New Bibliography of the 'Eikon Basilike'*, (Oxford Bibliographical Society, New Series, III, 1950), Frontispiece and Appendix VI.

The Explanation of the EMBLEME.

Ponderibus genus omne mali, probrisq; gravatus,
Vixq; ferenda ferens, Palma ut Depressa, resurgo.

Though clogg'd with weights of miseries
Palm-like Depress'd, I higher rise.

Ac, velut undarum Fluctûs Ventiq;, furorem
Irati Populi Rupes immota repello.
Clarior è tenebris, cœlestis stella, corusco.
Victor et æternùm–felici pace triumpho.

And as th'unmoved Rock out-brave's
The boist'rous Windes and rageing waves:
So triumph I. And shine more bright
In sad Affliction's Darksom night.

Auro Fulgentem rutilo gemmisq; micantem,
At curis Gravidam spernendo calco Coronam.

That Splendid, but yet toilsom Crown
Regardlessly I trample down.

Spinosam, at ferri facilem, quo Spes mea, Christi
Auxilio, Nobis non est tractare molestum.

With joie I take this Crown of thorn,
Though sharp, yet easie to be born.

Æternam, fixis fidei, semperq;–beatam
In Cœlos oculis Specto, Nobisq; paratam.

That heav'nlie Crown, already mine,
I view with eies of Faith divine.

Quod Vanum est, sperno; quod Christi Gratia præbet
Amplecti studium est: Virtutis Gloria merces.

I slight vain things; and do embrace
Glorie, the just reward of Grace.

G.D.

Τὸ Χρ̃ οὐδὲν ἠδίκησε τὴν πόλιν, δὸς τὸ Κάππα.

26. BMC 45   1671
From S. Clarke, *A True and Full Narrative of those two Never to be Forgotten Deliverances*. Based on the much-copied 'Double Deliverance' (1621) (BMC 41–7; George, *English Caricature*, I. plate 3), this much cruder version is a typical example of plagiarism. It adds the Great Fire of 1666 to the defeat of the Armada and the foiling of the Gunpowder Plot.

27. BMC 1067 (1681)
A strip cartoon history of the Popish Plot up to the execution of Viscount Stafford (29 Dec. 1680).

28. BMC 1080 (1680)

Promoted by Roger L'Estrange, this argued that the Dissenters, in league with the Papists, were plotting to overthrow Church and crown, as in the 1640s. An early example of what became a Tory cliché.

THE COMMITTEE; or Popery in Masquerade.

THE EXPLANATION.

Behold Here, in This Piece, the *Plague*, the *Fate*
Of a *Seditious Schism* in Church, and State:
Its *Rise*, and *Progress*; with the dire *Event*
Of a *Blind Zeal*, and a *Pack'd Parliament*.
It was *This Medly* that Confounded All;
This damn'd *Concert* of *Folly* and *Cabal*,
That Ruin'd us: For ye must know, that *Fools*
Are but *State-Engines*; *Politicians Tools*
Ground to an Edg, to *Hack*, and *Hew* it out;
Till by *dull Sots Knaves Ends* are brought about.
Think on't, my Masters; and if e're ye see
This Game play'd o're again, then Think of Me.

You'l say *This Print's* a *Satyr*, Against *Whom*?
Those that Crown'd *Holy Charles* with *Martyrdom*.
By the same rule the *Scripture* you'l Traduce,
For saying *Christ* was *Crucifi'd* by th' *Jews*:
Nay, and their *Treasons* too agreed in *This*;
By *Pharisees Betray'd*, and with a *Kiss*;
Conscience, the *Cry*; *Emanuel* was the *Word*;
The *Cause*, the *Gospel*; but the *Plea*, the *Sword*.

[A] Now lay your Ear close to That Nest of *Heads*.
Look, don't ye see a *Streaming Ray*, that sheds
A Light from the *Cabal* down to the *Table*;
To inspire, and Push on an *Enthusiast Rabble*?
In *That Box* sits a *Junto* in Debate.
Upon their *Sovereigns*, and *Three Kingdoms* Fate:
They're *Hot*, and *Loud* enough. Attend 'um pray e,
From point to point; and tell us what they say.

Is it Resolv'd then that the *King must Down*?
Not for a *World*; we'l only take his *Crown*:
He shall have *Caps*, and *Knees* still; and the Fame
Of a *fair Title*, and *Imperial Name*:
But for the *Sword*; the Power of *War*, and *Peace*;
Life, and *Death*; and such *Fooleries* as These;
We'l beg *These Baws out selves*: And Then, in Course,
What cannot be Obtain'd by *Prayer*, we'l *Force*.
It *Rests*, cow, only; by what *Arts*, and *Friends*,
Methods, and *Instruments*, to gain *These Ends*.

First, make the *People* Sure; and That must be
By *Pleas* for *Conscience*, *Common Liberty*:
By which Means, we secure a *Popular Voice*
For *Knights*, and *Burgesses*, in the Next *Choyce*.
If we can yet an *All*, *Then*, to *Sit in*
Tell we *Dissolve our Selves*, the work's *Half done*

In the mean while, the *Pulpits*, and the *Presses*
Must ring of *Popery*, *Grievances*, *Addresses*,
Plots of all Sorts, *Invasions*, *Massacres*,
Troops under Ground, *Plague-Plaisters*, *Cavaliers*:
Till, Mad with *Spite*, and *Jealousie*, the Nation
Cry out, as One Man, for a *Reformation*.

Having thus gain'd the *Rabble*; it must be our
Next Part, the *Common-Council* to Secure:
And Then; let *King*, *Law*, *Church*, and *Court-Cabal*,
Unite, and do their *Worst*; we'l Stand 'um All.
Our Design's *This*; to Change the *Government*;
Set up our *Selves*; and do't by a *Parliament*.
And This t' effect, needs only *Resolution*;
We'l leave the *Tumults* to do *Execution*.
The *Popish Lords* must Out, *Bishops* must *Down*;
Strafford must *Dye*; and *Then*, have at the *Crown*.
We will not leave the *King*, *One Minister*;
The *House*, *One Member*; but what *We Prefer*:
No nor the *Church*, *One Levite*; Down they go:
We, and the *'Prentices* will have it so.

[B] This was scarce sooner *Said*, then the thing
For upstarts *Little Isaac*, in the Room
Of *Loyd Gourney*, with a *Sword* in's hand;
The *Ensign* of his *New-usurpt Commands*:
Out of his Mouth, a *Label*. to be True
To the Design of the *Caballing Crew*:
[C] His *Holiness* at's Elbow; Heart'ning on,
A Motly *Schism*; Half-Pope, Half-Puritan
Who, while they talk of *Union*, bawl at *Rome*;
Revolt, and set up Popery at Home.

[D] Now, bring your Eye down to the *Board*; and
Th' *Agreement* of that Blest *Fraternity*:
Covenanters All; and by *That Holy Band*
Sworn Enemies to th' *Establisht Law* o' th' *Land*.
These are the Men that *Plague* all *Parliaments*,
For the *Impossible Expedients*
Of making *Protestant Dissenters*, *One*,
By *Acts* of *Grace*, or *Comprehension*:
When; by their very *Principles*, each other
Thinks himself *Bound* to *Persecute his Brother*.
They never *Did*; they never *Can* *Unite*
In any *one Point*; but t' *o're throw* the *Rest*;
Nor *consult* th' *Intent of Their Debate*
To be *Religious*; but t' *embroyl* the *State*;

Ill Accidents, and *Humours* to improve,
Under the fair Pretexts of *Peace*, and *Love*;
To serve the Turn of an *Usurping Power*.
But read their *Minutes*, and *They'l* tell ye More.

[E] Take a view, next, of the Petitioners.
But why, (you'l say) like *Beasts* to th' *Ark*, in *Pairs*?
Not t' expose the *Quaker*, and the *Maid*,
(By *Lust* to those *Brutalities* betray'd)
As if those *two Sects* more addicted stood
To *Mares*, and *Whelps*, then other *Flesh* and *Blood*:
No, But they're coupl'd *Here*, only to tell
The *Harmony* of their *Reforming Zeal*.

[F] Now wash your Eyes, and see their Secretarius
Of *Uncouth Visage*; Manners most *Nefarious*,
Plac'd betwixt *Pot* and *Pipe*, with *Pen* and *Paper*;
To shew that he can *Scribble*, *Tope*, and *Vapour*:
Beside him, (craving Blissing) a *Sweet Babby*;
(Save it!) the very Image of the *Daddy*!
He deals in *Sonnets*, *Articles*, takes *Notes*,
Frames *Histories*, *Impeachments*, enters *Votes*,
Draws *Narratives*, (for *Four Pound*) very well;
But then, 'tis *Forty more*, to Pass the *Seal*.
Beside his Faculty, at a *Dry Bob*,
That brings him many a comfortable Job.

[G] Mark, Now, Those *Club-men*; That Tumultuous
Crowd, *Bible*, *Magna Charta*, under Foot!
Those *Banners*, *Trophies*; and the *Execrable*
Rage, and Transports of an *Incensed Rabble*!
Here, the *Three States* in *Chains*; and *There*, the Head
Of a *Good King*, by *Rebels murthered*.
And all this while, the *Creatures* of *Those* Knaves,
That blew the Coal, themselves, the greatest Slaves.
What Devil could make Men Mad, to This Degree?
Only *mistaken Zeal*, and *Jealousie*.
Liberty, *Conscience*, *Popery*, the *Pretence*;
Rapine, *Blood*, *Sacrilege*, the *Consequence*.

[H] Let's *Cross* the way, Now, to the *Doctors* Side.
'Tis a good, pretty Girl, that holds his *Head*! (on
What's his Disease, *Sweet Heart*? Nay. That's a Questi-
His Stomach's Foul, perhaps, 'tis *It Dissolvers*
Best 'tis a mercy, 'twou'd Evacuate away;
Here's *Canons*, *Surplices*, *Apocrypha*!
Look what a Loosy stony lice of Common-Prayer.
Ay, but the *Crisis* in *Baptism*, that lies There?

O, how he *Reach't*; and still, as I provok'd him, (him!
He'd Heave for Life; 'twas Ten to One I had Choakt
Nay verily; This *Stuff*, in *Holder-forth*,
May be as much as a mans *Life* is worth.

How Do ye Sir? Why some what more at Ease,
Since I've Discharg'd these *Legal Crudities*.
But if your Stomach be *so extremely Nice*;
What Course do ye take? O, I have Good Advice;
There's not a man in the whole Club, but Joyns
The *Poll'cal*, you must know, keeps me alive;
Sequester'd Livings are *Preservatives*!
But for the *Sovereign Remedy* of all,
The *Only*, *never-failing Cordial*;
There 'tis upon *That Shelf*; *That Composition*
Th' *Assembly* Took, it self, in my *Condition*.
The Tears of Widows, Orphans Hearts, and Blood
They made their *daily Drink*, their *daily Food*:
Behold our *Christian Cannibol's Oblation*,
To auspicate their *Moloch Reformation*.

[I] Well! But what means *This Excremental Swarm*
Of *Human Insects*? How they *Fret*, and *Storm*;
Grin at the *Vanity*, and yet for all this *Pother*,
At the same Time, ly *teizing one another*.
Alas! 'Tis too, too true. you've Hit my Grief;
And there's no Help, no Help for't; no Relief.
While *They* joyn'd *Hands* with *Us*, against the *Crown*,
And *Church*; How sweetly the Lords work went on!
But when we came to plant our *Directory*,
Bless me, what *Freaks* they play'd! you know the Story.
Oh! of *themselves*, they're come a *Viperous Breed*;
Begot in Discord, and *brought up* with *Blood*.
'Twas *We* that *gave 'um* Life, Credit, and Name;
Till the *Ungrateful Brats* devour'd their *Dam*.

What could ye look for else? For 'tis *Dominion*,
That you do all contend for, not Opinion.
If you'l have any Government; then say,
Which Party shall Command, and *which* Obey.
Power is the thing ye both Affect, and Hate.
Every one would, ye *Cannot*, All be Great.
This is, in short, the *Sum* of the Contest:
Still He that's *Up*, 's an *Eye-sore* to the Rest.
Presbytery breeds *Worms*: This *Maggot-Fry*
Is but the *Spawn* of *Lawless Liberty*.
Licence, it like a *Sea-Breach* to your Grounds;
Suffer but *One Flaw*, the whole *Country Drowns*.

LONDON: Printed by *Mary Clark*, for *Henry Brome*, at the *Gun* in St. *Pauls* *Church-yard*. 1680. 15 Aprill.

29. BMC 1085   Nov. 1680
One of several prints (see also BMC 1072, 1084) of the pope-burning pageants organized by the Exclusionists on 17 November (Queen Elizabeth's accession day). Towzer is L'Estrange. The 'meal tub' refers to an ill-fated Catholic attempt to concoct a 'Presbyterian plot' by 'finding' letters in a meal tub. See S. Williams, 'The Pope-burning processions of 1679–81', *Journal of the Warburg and Courtauld Institutes*, XXI. (1958); Miller, *Popery and Politics*, pp. 183–7.

30. BMC 1110   March 1681   S. College
This shows the full gamut of anti-Catholic stereotypes and denounces L'Estrange and the High Church parsons as crypto-Papists. It reflects the Whigs' confidence on the eve of the last Exclusion Parliament. College was executed on a dubious treason charge later in the year: see George, *English Caricature*, I. 56–7 and plate 16.

31. BMC 1112   March 1681
    Produced just after Charles II had dissolved the last Exclusion Parliament, this concentrates its attack on the Tories rather than the Papists. 'Forty-one is here again', raising fears of another civil war, was the Tories' favourite slogan.

THE TIME-SERVERS: Or, A TOUCH OF THE TIMES.
Being a DIALOGUE between
Tory, Towzer, and Tantivee,
At the News of the Dissolution of the
Late Worthy Parliament at Oxford.

The EXPLANATION of the FIGURE.

Reader, here is presented to thy View
The true Effigies of a *Popish* Crew:
An Irish *TORY*, and a *Popish Priest*,
And the Cur *TOWZER* (to make up the jest)
All on the speed for *Rome*; *TORY* o'ertakes
The Clergy, and, his Company thus bespeaks,
Spur on (Sir *Priest*) Spur on, The day's our own,
If that a *Papist* comes t'injoy the Crown:
The *Parliament's* dissolv'd, the Coast is clear,
No other Obstacles we need to fear:
Macnamarra cursed be, and *Harris* too,
That lets the world know what it should not do,
In spight of all their tricks let us but joyn
Our Forces, all is ours, my life for thine.
Do you but prate and write, let me alone
To make the way for a *Succession*
By other means, and our Attempts shall be
Rewarded both with wealth and dignity;
Act with thy Brains, and I'll act with my Sword,
Thou shalt a Bishop be, and I a Lord.
When that day comes---With that the *Priest* spurs on,
Bauling (at every jog) *Succession*:
Let things go how they will, better or worse,
The Saddle should be laid on the right Horse;
I'm for the true Successor's constant sway
O'th' *British Scepter*, let the world say Nay:
Let *Care* himself, and his *Fanatick* Crew,
Say what they will, *Princes* must have their due.
Princes must have their rights, *Religion*
Must always pay its homage to the *Crown*:
'Tis my belief, I know no *Deity*
On Earth to be ador'd, but Soveraignty.
The question lies not, how we are t'Obey
Or Suffer, but whose right it is to Sway
The *Scepter*, They'r the right, the duty's ours,
To be obedient to the Higher Powers.

Conscience, that silly thing, that keeps in awe
The trembling *Vulgar*, must not check the Law;
The Laws of *Empire* are most sacred things,
People will have their due, and why not *Kings*.
The times were glorious, and the Nation flourish'd,
When th'*English Church* by *Mother Church* was nourish'd.
But since 'twas *weaned* from her Breasts, we find
How She is wasted, languished and pin'd;
Revenue's gone, Promotions scarce and few,
Not half enough for the *Tantivee*-Crew.
The times must mend, we must reform the *State*,
And I will do't, or sink under my Fate:
Winged with all the haste I can, I come
To pay my Homage to the *Church of Rome*;
Towzer run on, and *TORY* clear the way,
Till I a *Myter* get I will not stay.
And then he hum'd himself, and spur'd again
A full *Tantivee* speed with a loose rein,
And bended Body; *Towzer* trips before
(As brisk now as he was in times of Yore)
And whiles the other bawl's *Succession*,
This barks and yelps nothing but *Forty-One*.
A cunning Cur to think to drown our fears
Of future dangers with forgotten Years:
Well thus they troop together till they come
Unto the confines of desired *Rome*,
And here the *Holy-Father* ready stands
With smiling Countenance, and reared Hands
Lift up to bless them, In the one is Gold,
The other doth a gorgeous *Myter* hold,
These (as the guerdons of their merits) he
Allures them with; And thus betray'd are we
'Twixt our known Enemies, and feigned friends,
Ayming by serving thus their own base ends,
Us into *Popish Slavery* to bring,
Which God in Heaven prevent.---*God Save the King.*

FINIS.

London, Printed for *W. H.* and are to be Sold by R. *Janeway* in Pater-Noster-Row. 1681.

32. BMC 1126   1683
Frontispiece to E. Pettit, *Visions of the Reformation*. This repeats the allegation that the Dissenters are doing the Papists' work for them.

THE VISIONS OF THOROUGH REFORMATION.

The Royall Armes doth Presbyter deface:
To Paint the Comon Wealth's upon the place
Thus to Reform from Popery, he draw's
A Cross; the Comon Seal to th good Old Cause;
Thus when the Kingdom turns a Comon wealth
The Imperiall Crown will be the Popes by Stealth.

33. BMC 1127   1683
Another print evoking memories of the Interregnum and playing on fears of republicanism and military rule.

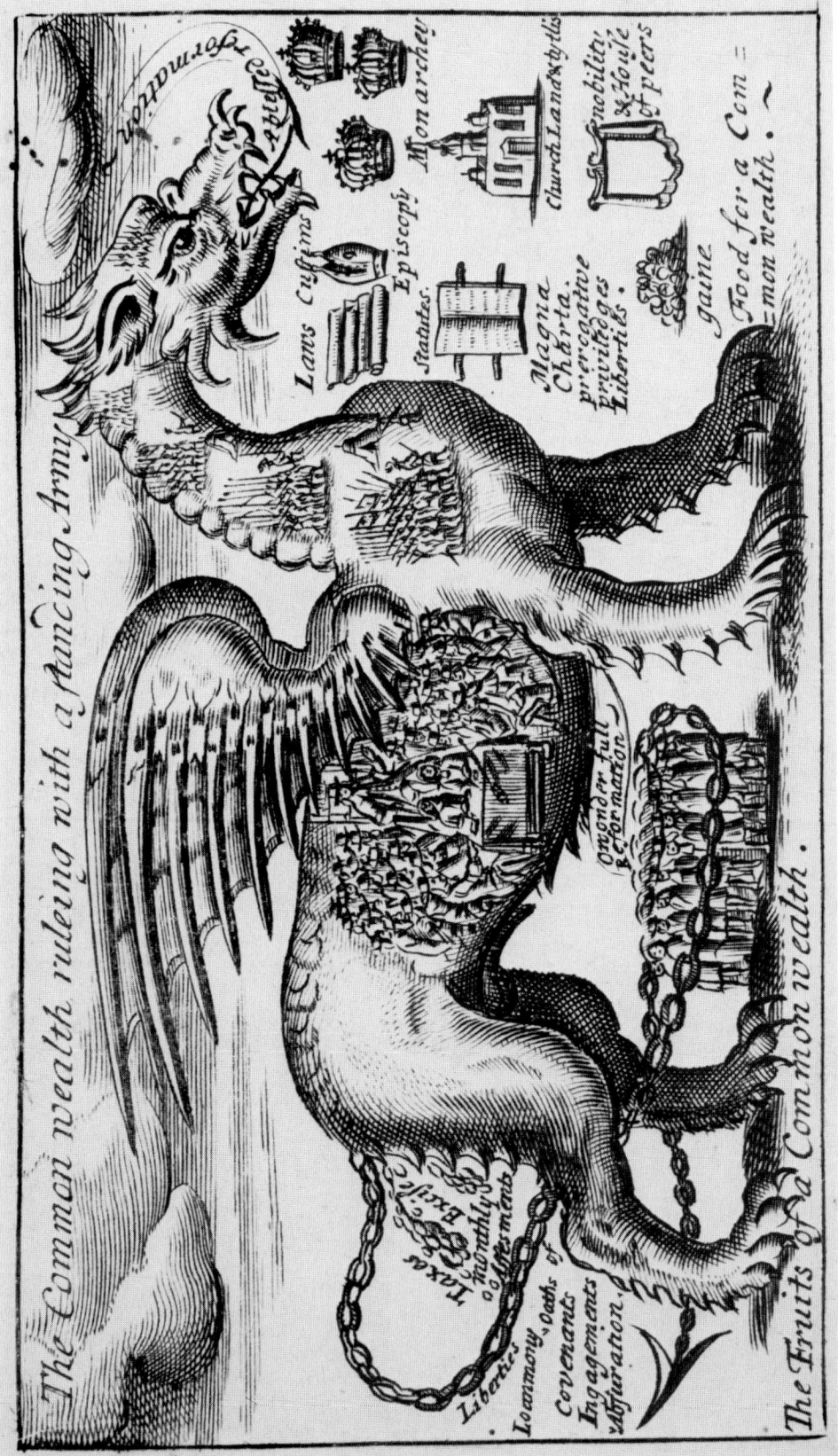

34. BMC 1162   1688
A medal on the birth of the allegedly spurious Old Pretender. The toleration which James II offered the Dissenters is depicted as a Trojan horse.

35. BMC 1168   1688
Portraits of the seven bishops prosecuted by James II and acquitted. Note the text from Revelation.

36. BMC 1186   (1688/9)
    Partly allegorical representation of the Glorious Revolution.

37. BMC 1339 (1699)
From F. Bugg, *Some Reasons . . . why the Quakers Principles Should be Examined and Censured or Suppressed*. Bugg alleged that the Quakers did not observe the conditions imposed by the Toleration Act and claimed virtual immunity from the laws. Unusual in dealing with Dissenters, when most prints were concerned with the battles within the Church.

38. BMC 1465   1706
   Inspired by an inn sign on the theme 'The Church in Danger' this argues that any harm that befalls the Church will be caused by its own follies and weaknesses.

The High-Church Hieroglyphick

Represented in the Sign of the

EMBLEME,

Put up at an Inn in STOKE by Naland, in Suffolk.

An EXPLANATION of the EMBLEME.

Behold the *Church*, which some Men say has stood,
Unmov'd from Times before the mighty Flood:
Its Basis laid in the Auspicious Reign
Of that most Glorious Murdering Monarch *Cain*;
By Murdering *Levites* then Possess'd and Rul'd,
Whose Progeny, till now, the People Gull'd.
  Its vast Foundation to great Depths they fix,
Down to the very Banks of Sulph'rous *Stix*;
Whose Fiery Waves with Hideous Noise do Roar,
Admit no Bounds, but warp away the Shore:
Its Spires above the Clouds they Proudly rear,
Cover'd about by *Demons* of the Air.
This is *High-Church*, as its *Devotes* her call;
This is the *Church* you see enclin'd to Fall.
  Stay, Passenger, a while the EMBLEME view,
Say, Is't a *Church* that's *False*, or One that's *True*?
If *True*, she's out of Danger of a Fall;
'Gainst her the Power of *Hell* can ne'er prevail:
If *False*, as we have by Experience found,
Blest be the Hands shall rase her to the Ground.

Prepost'rous Sight! That *Devils* shou'd Invade,
And Spoil the Work that their own Hands have made.
Yes, Spectator, Prepost'rous is the SIGN,
That those who Built the *Church* should UNDERMINE:
'Tis not *Infernal De'ils*, nor those that Fly,
But its own Sins has weigh'd its Spires awry.
  Next view its Sons, the *Buttresses* o'the *Dome*,
How they with Zeal to its Assistance come;
With Brawny Shoulders strive to underprop,
And keep the vast declining Fabrick Up;
The *High-Tantivy-Priests*, the *Tacking-Elves*,
Who would, to Ruin *England*, Damn themselvs.
  See the *Non-Cons*, and *Moderate-Churchmen* Laugh,
To find themselves, by *High-Church* Fall, more safe.
Thus *Virtue* thrives when *Vice* is most suppres't,
And *Hell* restrain'd, adds Numbers to the Blest.
  Let *High-Church* stand, or let it tumble down,
Its Peoples Folly in their Motto's shown,
Who take a *Rising* for a *Setting* Sun.

LONDON, Printed in the Year 1706.

39. BMC 1494   1709
On the old theme that the Whigs are continuing the practices of the Parliamentarians, undermining authority in Church and state. Note Samuel Clarke, preaching against the Trinity. The identity of E.P. is not entirely clear – possibly Shaftesbury.

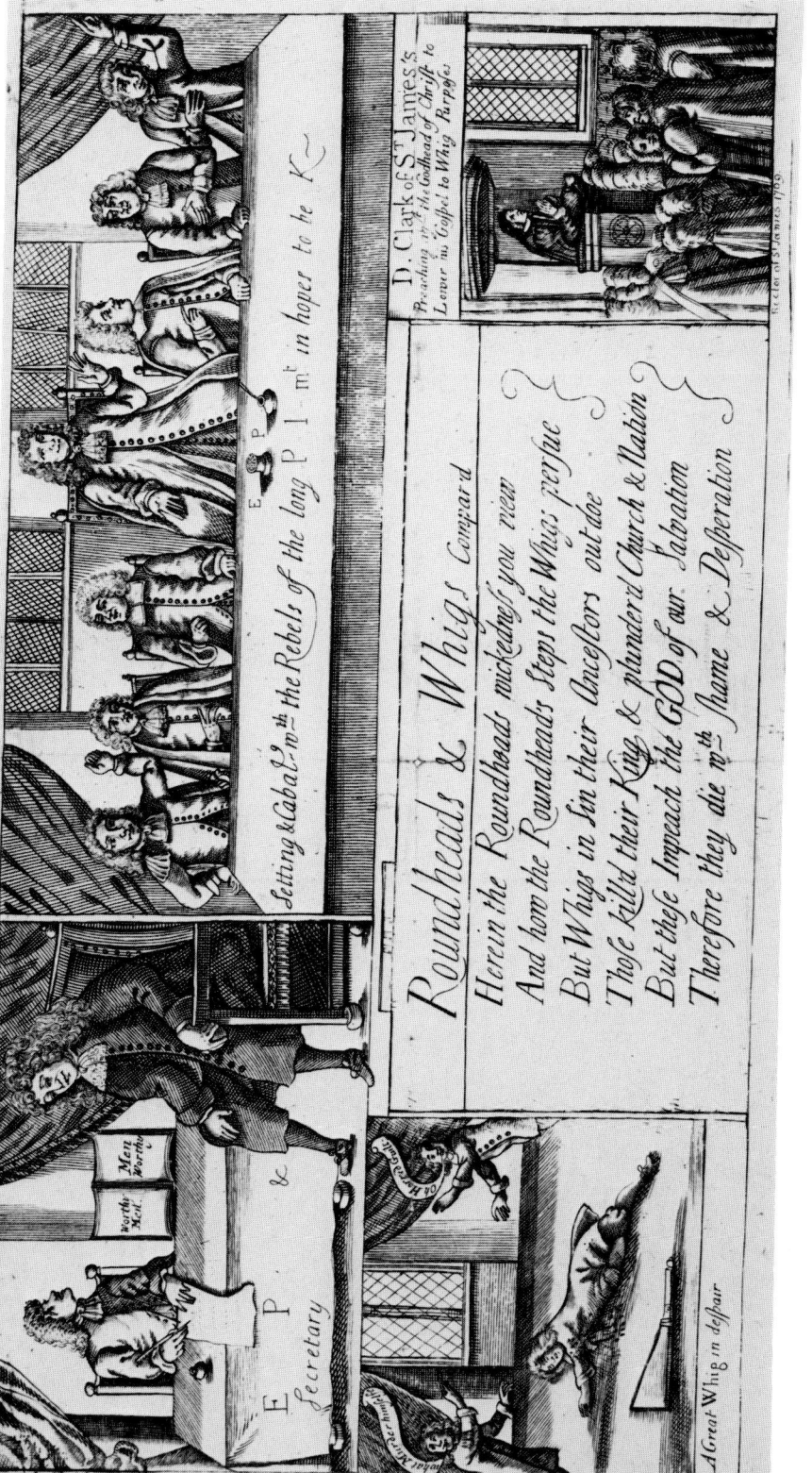

40. BMC 1496   1709
Whig/Low Church cartoon equating High Church principles with Popery, Jacobitism and tyranny in Church and state. Perkin is the Pretender. Wooden shoes symbolise the poverty of the people in absolutist France. See also BMC 1495, 1498.

Needs must when the DEVIL drives:
or, AN EMBLEM
Of what we must expect, if High-Church gets uppermost.

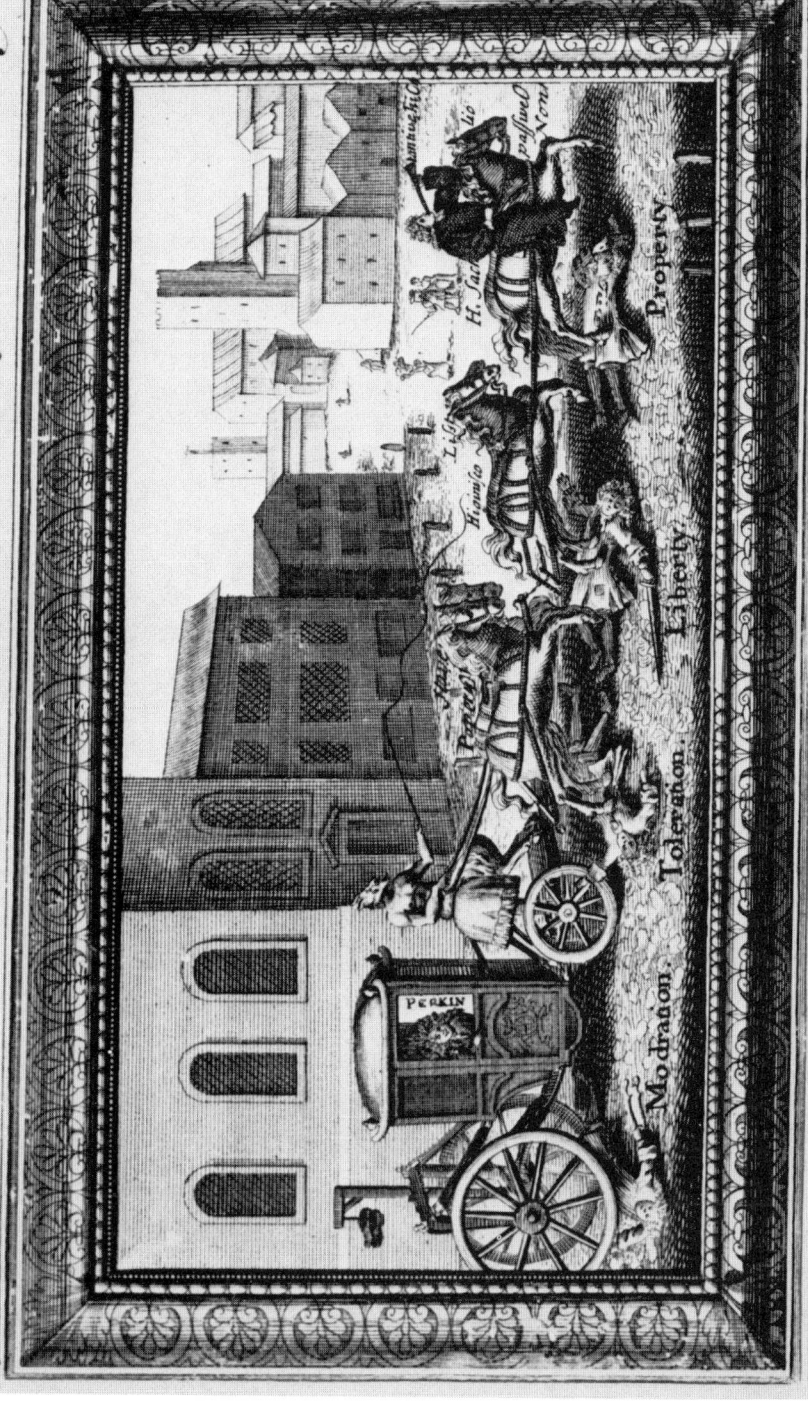

41. BMC 1497   1709
Tory/High Church riposte to *40*. The Prayer Book is trampled underfoot by 'moderation' (i.e., heterodoxy or Latitudinarianism). The identification of Whiggery and rebellion is commonplace; less usual is the sympathetic reference to Strafford, Charles I's minister.

LIKE COACHMAN, LIKE CAUSE: OR, AN EMBLEM.

Of what we must expect, if Low-Church gets uppermost.

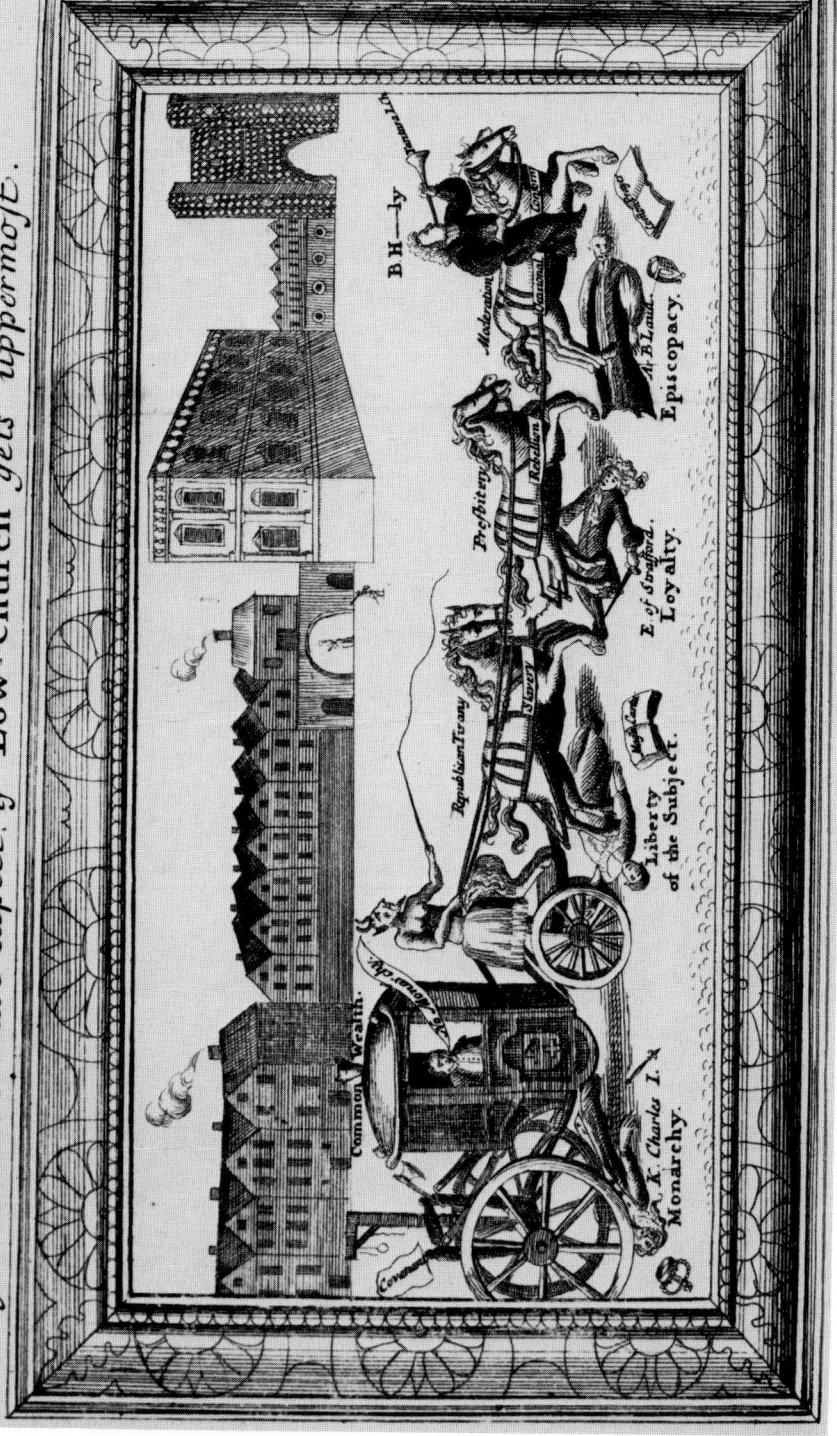

42. BMC 1502   1709
On the same theme as *41*. Hoadly and the Dissenters wish to bring the Church into line with Salters' Hall (where Presbyterians and Congregationalists met).

The Schismatical attack o'ye CHURCH Besieg'd by ye Ephesian Beast

Lead on your Beast for the attack prepare,
Ye growling Wolv's who Shepherds clothing wear;
That Pious Men with weeping Eyes may See
S.t Pauls, at last, with Salter's Hall agree:

But Stand to't Churchmen, guard the Sacred Door,
Beat back the Monster, and Exert your Pow'r;
For if the Beast prevails, too late you'll find
A Common Wealth come Sneaking in behind.

43. BMC 1503   1709
A more personal attack on Hoadly, referring (as so often) to Hoadly's deformed leg.

Guess att my Meaning.

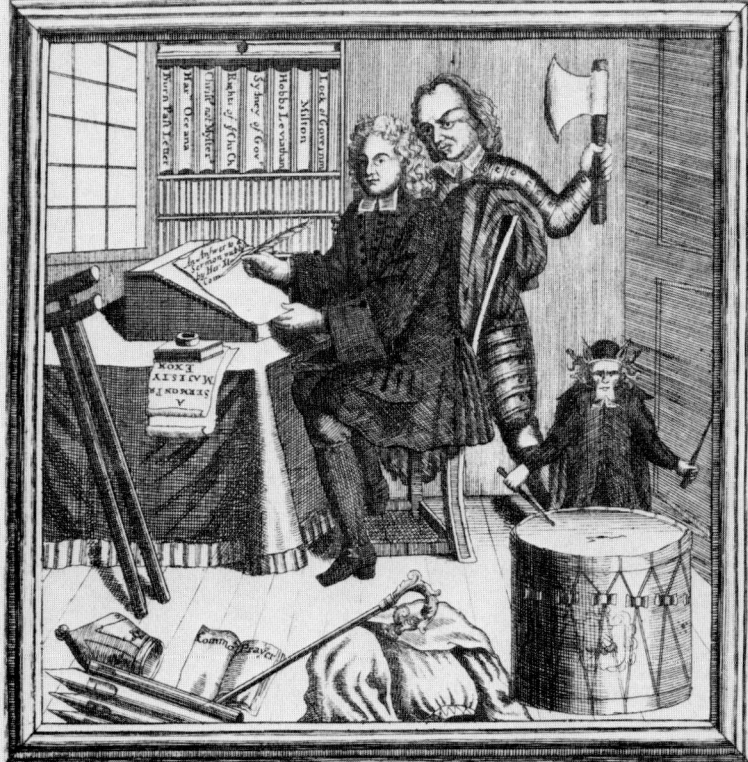

There is a man ye present Age think fit
Amongst our Loyal Bishops rank to sit
A Cripled Priest whose Intellects are lame
As his Supporters, noxcious as his name
Who gives each Toppick ye he treats such touches
As like himself must be upheld by Crutches
A brave Defender of the Establish'd Church
As ever left Her Doctrine in the lurch

But I'm perswaded such a Crooked-Stick
As ne'er will gain an English Bishoprick
And may they ne'er obtain our Soveraignes Favour
That dare be guilty of such Rude-Behaviour
As to confront the Doctrine She esteems
The only Medium free from all Extreams
As he has done, as every Child can tell
That Boasts in b'ing an Anticheverell

Yet buy the Emblem, ther's a great deal in't
Tis Ænigmatical, A Riddle-Print.

S Fredericus Leopold excudit. Geneva.

44. BMC 1505   1709
An attack on Low Churchmen, only half committed to the Church's interests and sympathetic to Dissent. For an earlier similar print, see BMC 1231.

A British Janus
Angliçe a Timeserver.

Since Moderation is so much in vogue,
And few can tell a Trimmer from a R——;
I am perswaded such a Print as this,
Thus modell'd and contriv'd can't be amiss.
At such a juncture, such a time as this,
When to be loyal is esteem'd a fault,
Obedience hist at, Scripture sett at nought,
And ye reverse for pure sound doctrine taught.
I mean by them this picture doth resemble,
Who preach not half so fine as they dissemble.
Of Heterogeneous parts as opposite,
Compos'd, as darkness to Meridian light.
Made up of halves that can no more agree,
Than Regal pow'r and Independency.
A British Janus with a double face,
A Monster of a strange Gigantick Race:
His head half Mitre, and half hat doth bear;
His looks are sainted, and refin'd his air.
Not more preposterous in his black & white,
Than the true semblance of an Hypocrite.
Always Conformist to the strongest Party;
Always deceitful, Ever more unhearty.
The Moderate Man ne'er yet a Martyr dy'd;
But tack'd about, & chose the strongest side.
Always recanted in the time of trial;
Is ever best extempore at denial.
Scorne to be moderate then in any thing,
But where to be immoderate is a sin.
In eating, drinking, and such things as these
Be moderate, as moderate as you please.
But in Religion there's no Medium. No!
Who is not truly zealous, is not so.
Glory to be esteem'd an High-c——h Man:
Let them prove Low-c——h true c——h, if they can.
Zeal for the c——h's Cause a Crown will gain;
And Martyrdom for He'ven's an easy pain.
Dare to be true, tho' in a suff'ring time;
A Bare Denial then's a Double Crime.

45. BMC 1513   (1710)
    Crude but effective illustration of Sacheverell's popularity.

THE Modern IDOL or Kiss my A-se is no Swearing

These Figures act a Tory Farce,
Quite mad to kiss the D—ter's A-se.
His br—ches are already down,
In no small danger is his Gown.
He Peers among the Fair, & Young;
While his right hand is lifted high,
The poor old Beldame to deny.

Tho' leaning on a stick, she come
With aged Zeal, and toothless gumm,
To kiss th' Ecclesiastick B-m.
See Misses hair, is torn off by Dol.
In his Tory, Rory, Glory,
Mark THE IDOL.

46. BMC 1521   1710
The destruction of Dr Burgess's Presbyterian chapel in Carey Street by the Sacheverell rioters.

47. BMC 1546   1710
A set of playing cards on the Sacheverell affair, including the Tory election triumph of 1710 and (six of hearts) the Duchess of Marlborough's fall from favour. The knave of hearts is the Whig son of the Archbishop of York, who presented the impeachment.

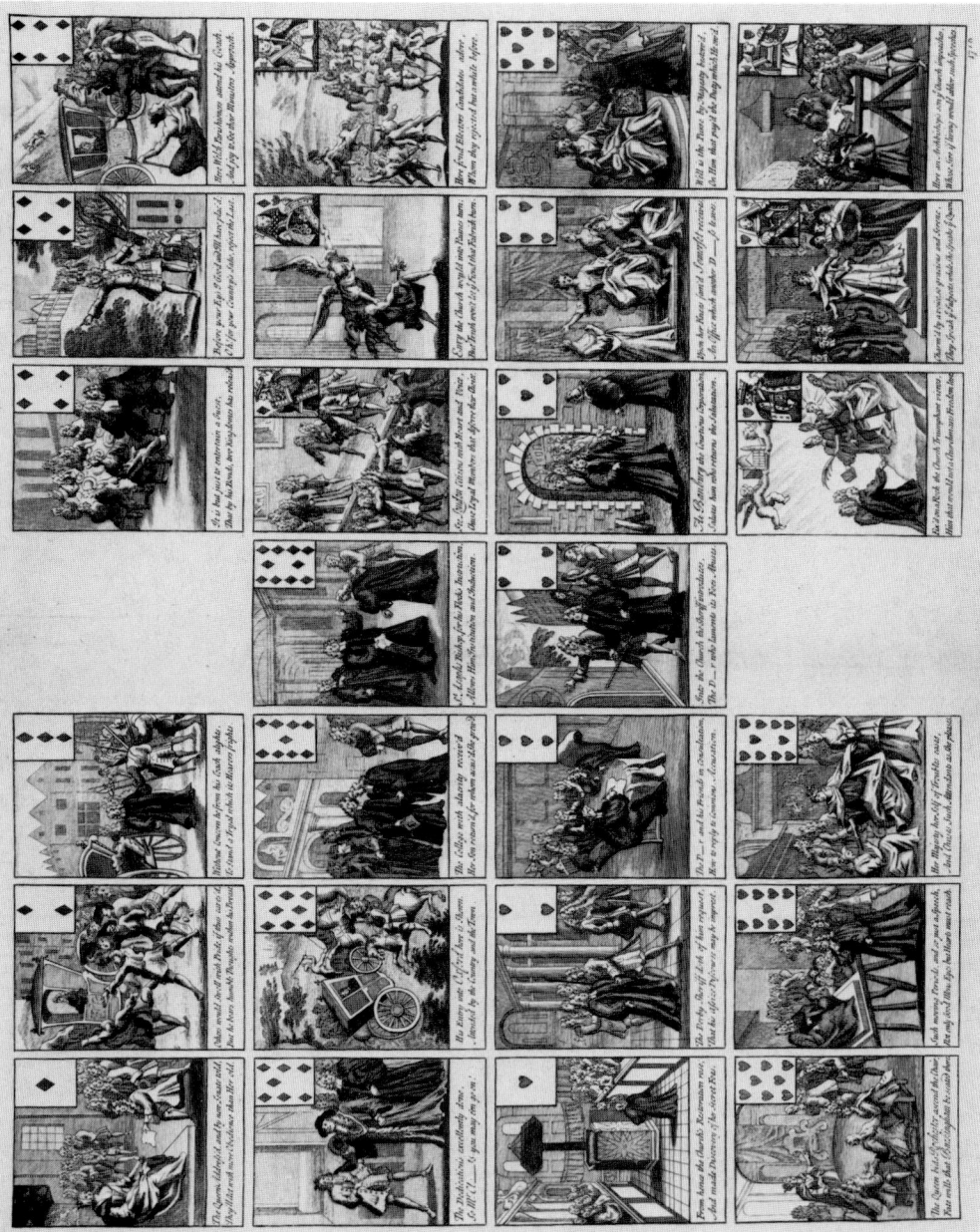

48. BMC 1775 (c.1725)
Expresses cynicism about the three learned professions. See also BMC 3761.

The TRIPLE PLEA.

Law, Physick, and Divinity,
Contend which shall Superior be.
The Lawyer pleads He is your Friend,
And will your Rights & Cause defend.
The Doctor swears (deny't who will)
That Life and Health are in his Pill.
The grave Divine, with Look demure,
To Penitents will Heaven assure.

But mark these Friends of ours & see
Where ends their great Civility.
Without a Fee, the Lawyer's Dumb;
Without a Fee, the Doctor Mum;
His Rev'rence says, without his Dues,
You must the Joys of Heaven lose.
Then be advis'd: In none confide;
But take Sound Reason for your Guide.

Sold by J. Jarvis, Bedford-Court Covent Garden.

49. BMC 2285   1736   W. Hogarth
See also BMC 8259.

50. BMC 7777   1790   After Woodward
    Note the hunting boots under the surplice.

"— And first — the Curate,
Humming and hawing to his drowsy herd."

51. BMC 2905   1747   W. Hogarth
    An illustration of prudential morality and the material advantages of church attendance. Although some are asleep, most are reading and singing, in contrast to *49*.

52. BMC 2823   Dec. 1746

'Orator' Henley was an ordained clergyman who opened his own church (the 'Oratory') in London, which provided both religious services of his own devising and lectures of an 'educational' nature. As he depended on admission fees, the need to attract customers drove him to lecture on bizarre and sensational topics. Despite his eccentricity, he avoided serious trouble until 1746, when his mockery of the government's poor showing against the rebels led to accusations of Jacobitism. See G. Midgley, *The Life of Orator Henley* (Oxford, 1973).

THE TEMPLE OF REBELLION.

H—y exalts his Voice, his Arms extends,
And Blasphemy & Treason madly blends.
The old Seducer, still to Traytors near,
Inspires his Eloquence, & checks his Fear:
A Scarlet Hat's the Lure—Shou'd chance—a Rope?
Why he'd be canoniz'd by Church & Pope:
Thus whilst he risks his Neck, their Spleen to feast,
His Rebel-Flock applaud their Zany-Priest:
But Shame will sure bedimm his brazen Face,
When Ketch prepares to give—The Coup de Grace.

Publish'd according to Act of Parliament December 10. 1746

53. BMC 2003 (1730s?)

54. BMC 2618   1744
One of two very similar versions, the other being BMC 2617. Among many other prints on this theme, see BMC 2269, 3753–4, 6153–4.

THE PLURALIST.

Mark, hov'ring here the fat Incumbent lies,
And like a Bird of Prey the Quarry Eyes.
No Sine Cure he, for nullfast Views engag'd,
Nor what can frustrate Chance assuage:
First let a Vicarage supply his want,
He nexts will sute a wealthy Prebend grant.

Rector next, that Honour's are too mean,
The Reverend Doctor longs to be a Dean:
The Deanery of Fortune kind afford,
At Court he cringes — to be made a Lord.
That Seat obtain'd, he still improves his Plan,
And dines at Lambeth with what's for the can.

Thus while in Wealth y well fed Prelate rolls,
Far too beneath his thoughts the Cure of Souls;
So Curates drudge the lazy Drone to serve,
Who seeks on Learning only fat to starve.
If still Monopolies were deem'd a Curse,
Pluralities are yet a Grievance worse.

1 Aug. 1744.

55. BMC 4236   1768
From an article in the *Oxford Magazine* about the 'risings' of various types of workers for higher wages.

The rising of the inferior Clergy.

56. BMC 2867   Oct. 1747
There are several versions of this print, suggesting a scramble among the bishops on the death of Archbishop Potter. In fact, Gibson refused to be considered in either 1737 or 1747 while Sherlock (mentioned in another version) also declined the primacy. The eventual choice was Herring, archbishop of York. See Sykes, *Gibson*, pp. 175–81, 384–6; *Dictionary of National Biography*, under Thomas Sherlock.

First Oars to L--m--th; or, who strives for Preferment.

Archbishop Potter died 10 Oct. 1747.

A Bp. Herring.

I.
AT *Lambeth* dwells as fame Reports,
A Priest of spotless Fame,
Some Annual Thousands swell his Worth,
And spread abroad his Name.

II.
From Sacred Crops his Coffers rise,
Yet who can Fate withstand?
His rival Tribe with envious Eyes
Behold the promis'd Land;

III.
Whilst Meagre Death at Distance waits,
Th' expecting Crowd attends,
Each strives to Grasp the gilded Bait,
And each his Vows thus sends:

IV.
Vouchsafe, great Jove! when Breath forsakes
This Mass of Sattin'd L--w--n,
Let me possess the self same Place,
The self same Triple Crown.

V.
Three M--i--t--r--'d Brethren, big with hope,
More eager than the rest,
Would fain be stil'd an *English* P--p--e,
And so commence high Priest.

VI.
Their various Consults all prepare,
Each Summons each his Friend,
Some fly to Int'rest, some to Pray'r,
T' attain their wish'd for End.

VII.
In this at length they all agree;
To Oars, my Friends to Oars,
Ambition calls, let's cross the *Thames*,
And Steer for *Lambeth* Shore.

VIII.
Who knows how soon kind Heav'n will please
It's Favours to dispose?
When Life's upon the Wing, 'tis time,
To know our Friends from Foes.

IX.
Their Measure's fix'd, the silent Night,
Befriends the close Design,
The Sacerdotal Robe's prepar'd,
The L--w--n and Sattin shine.

X.
Three Boats attend; each Enters in,
Unweildly in his Seat,
The Scyphs move gently on, but shake,
Beneath the holy VVeight.

XI.
With awkard Strokes the Clumsy Priests
Divide the liquid Wave,
Now Stare before, now look behind,
And haste the Prize to save.

XII.
H--a--l--y with headstrong Zeal inspir'd,
Vows he'll compleat the Work,
Whilst G--i--b--o--n Tugs and Toils in vain
T' o'ertake the furious T--a--r--k.
Herring

XIII.
Thus at *New-Market* have I seen,
Three founder'd Jades set out,
With Clumsy Riders on their Backs,
To scour the Plain about.

XIV.
The royal Plate adorns the Goal,
And Tempts the rider's Eyes,
But Horse and Man are so alike,
That neither gains the Prize.

57. BMC 5125   June 1773
This depicts Josiah Tucker, dean of Gloucester and (probably) Lord Rochford, a secretary of state. Such simony was rare: political considerations took precedence over financial in church preferments.

The Morning Visit

Dean MY Lord I hope your goodness will excuse
This early Visit, since my only views
Are centerd in the glory of your House.
And now have brought a trifle ——— for your Spouse
Of which I beg her kind acceptance ——— then
Rank me my Lord, amongst the happiest men.

Lord My rev'rend Dean I'm glad to see you now,
Early or late; or any time, I vow :
What news abroad, my rev'rend Dean, what news?
Something's behind ——— have you no trifling views
In which my Intrest can the least avail ———?

Dean Indeed, my Lord, there is a flying tale
That my good Lord of B———h declines so fast
With Age, and Gout, this fit will be his last.

Lord I know he's old, and cannot long be here:
But, rev'd Dean, you know ——— what 'tis a Year :
'Twill gain me friends ———

Dean ——— My Lord I know that's true,
And all the Intrest in my pow'rs your due
In future times the same shall me controul
My Friends ——— Estate ——— my Body, and my ———.

Lord 'Tis well my rev'rend Dean ——— all's very right ;
On these conditions you're put down to night,
You shall succeed ———

Dean ——— All grateful thanks are due :
My gratitude shall shine, my Lord ——— : my Lord adieu

Publish'd as the Act directs June 1775

58. BMC 6337 (c.1783)
Apart from providing a living for the younger sons of the nobility and gentry, the Church was also used to provide for disbanded army officers. For a similar complaint from the 1820s, see Cobbett, *Rural Rides*, II. 157–8.

59. BMC 8031   Dec. 1791   Woodward
    An unusually detailed satire on the nature of clerical promotions.

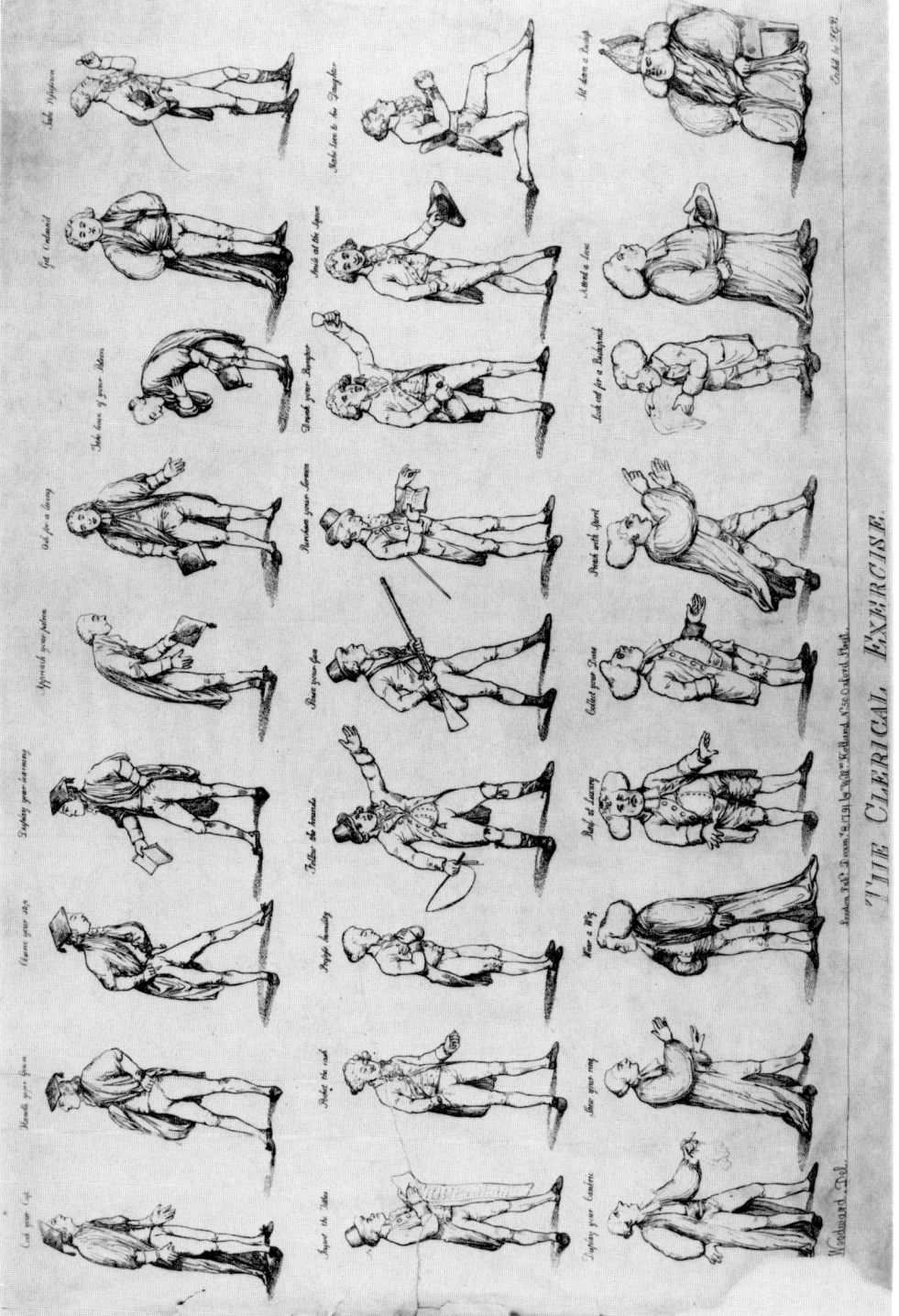

60. BMC 2474   Dec. 1741
One of numerous allegations that parsons and parish officials embezzled or drank away parish funds. For another example, see BMC 4804.

The Rev'rend Roſt-Prieſt with mirthful glee, | The Meager Reader graſps a Fowl his prey, | A Pariſh Feaſt, humbly Inſcribed to the
Toſſes the Glaſs to Church Proſperity. | Another, the Sly Warden doe's convey, | Church-Wardens, Veſtrymen, Queſtmen, and
His Jolly Clerk no leſs elated view, | Whilſt the Arch Beadle not to Spoil the Joke, | Pariſh Officers, by S'. Guzzledown Tearfowl.
Better to aim: the're then in a Pew. | Wraps the ſeiv'd Bottle underneath his Cloak.

61. BMC 5003   April 1772
    A fashionable churchman, from a volume of 'caricatures, macaronies and characters'.

62. BMC 5553   Sept. 1779   Gillray
Led by Archbishop Markham, the clergy show themselves interested only in avoiding work. The bishops' hostility to the American colonists during the War of Independence was often attacked by the Opposition.

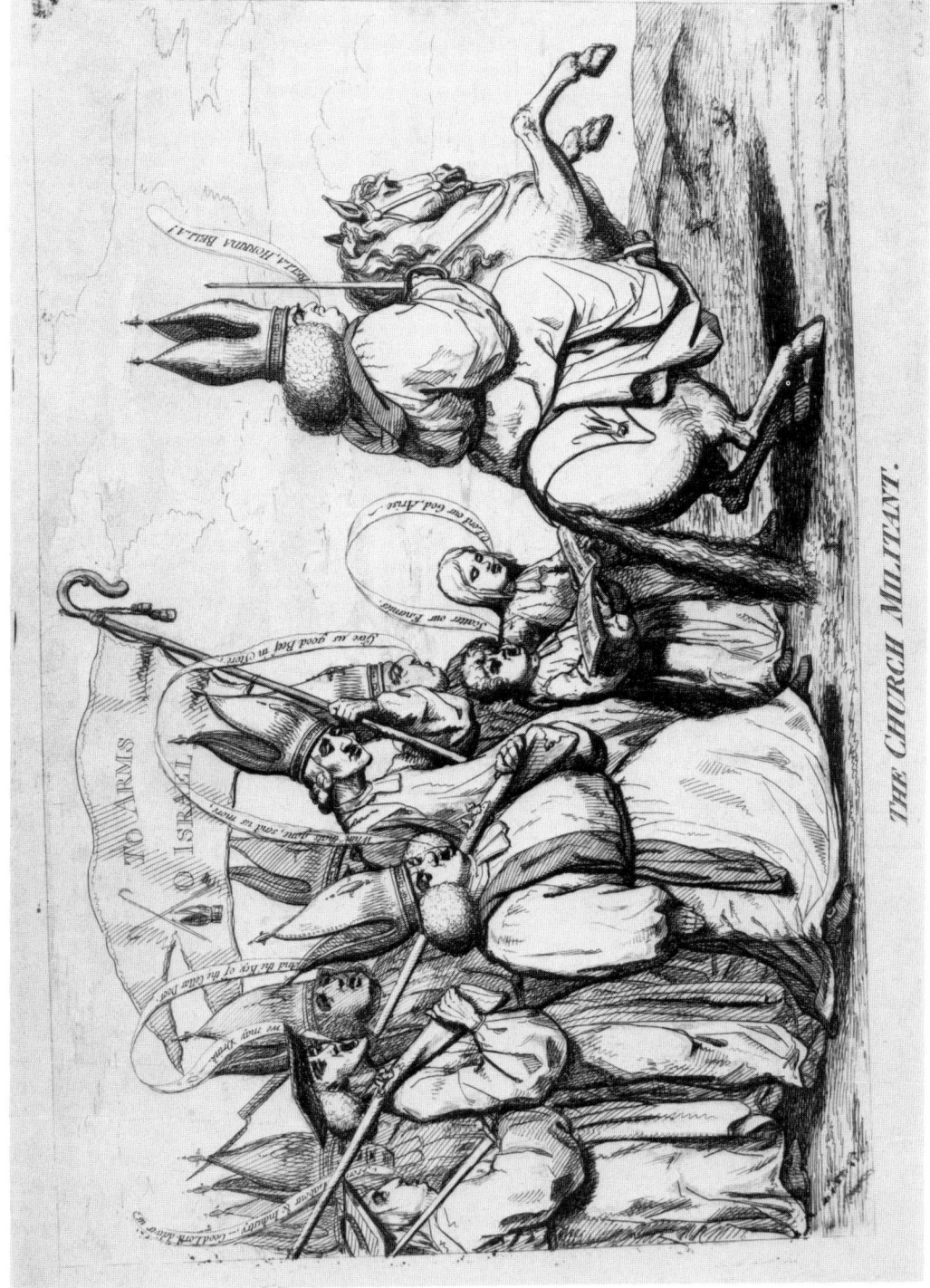

THE CHURCH MILITANT.

63. BMC 6130   Jan. 1782   (T. Colley?)
This print was said to be very popular 'among the vulgar': Stephens and George, *Catalogue*, V. 654. For another version, see BMC 3771.

64. BMC 1997   1733
This symbolic representation of the sanctity and antiquity of episcopacy appeared in the last edition of W. Cave, *Antiquitates Apostolicae*, first published in 1675. Such sentiments would appear archaic and even provocative in the Latitudinarian and anti-clerical 1730s.

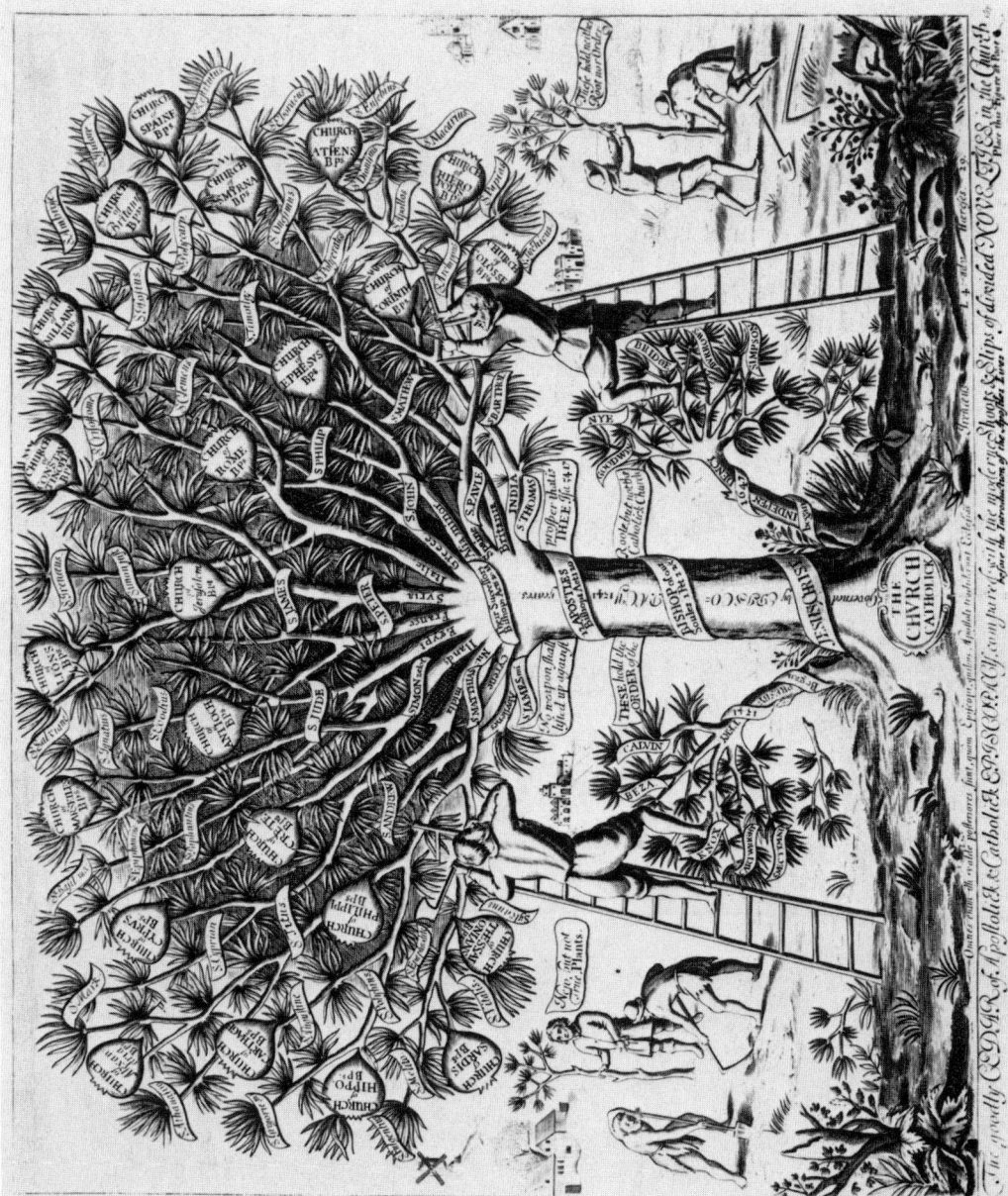

65. BMC 2149 1735

This attacks the High Church for its intolerance of the likes of Hoadly and Clarke and its clericalism. The clergy are shown trying to dominate the laity, especially through the church courts, while the state is seen as subservient to the Church (in the person of Gibson, nicknamed 'Codex' after his great work of canon law). This was an inversion of the natural order, like a man who was beaten by his wife (who would be mocked by a 'skimmington', a derisive cavalcade). The print was occasioned by Gibson's opposition to the elevation of Rundle, a Latitudinarian, to the bishopric of Gloucester. See Sykes, *Gibson*, pp. 155–60.

66. BMC 2280 (1736)
Another attack on Gibson for trying to raise the Church above the state. It refers to his organising the bishops' successful opposition in the Lords to the Quakers' Tithes Bill, which had government support. See Sykes, *Gibson*, pp. 163–75; Stephens and George, *Catalogue*, III, 196–8.

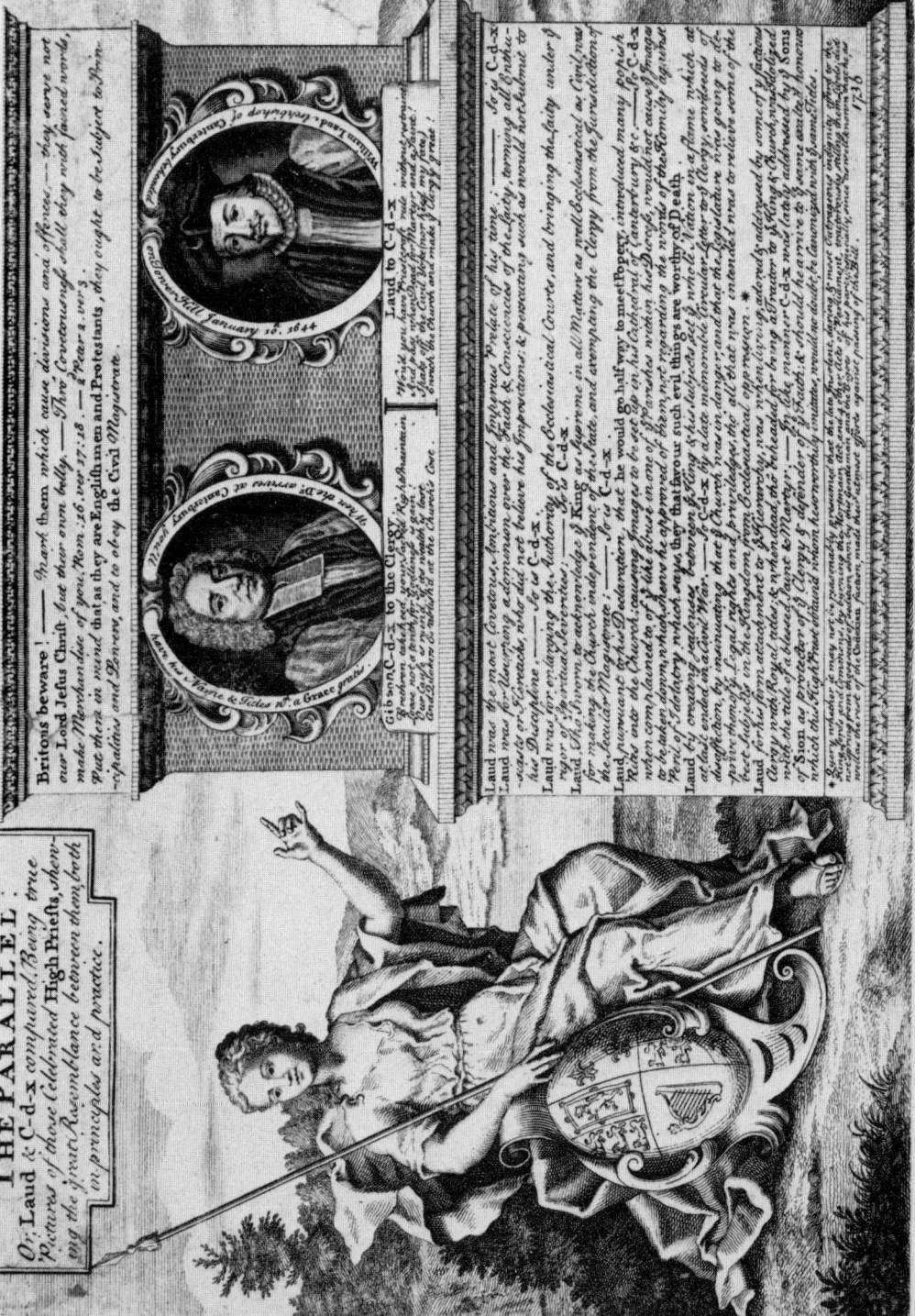

67. BMC 1262   (1719)

Misdated 1690 by Stephens. This refers to the debates among leading Presbyterians and Congregationalists about whether ordinands might be permitted to hold anti-Trinitarian opinions. This led, in effect, to the final breach between the two denominations.

68. BMC 4794 (c.1770)
   Very unusual in that it deals with Old Dissent, largely ignored by eighteenth-century caricaturists.

69. BMC 2425   (1739)   W. Hogarth
An attack on the early Methodists, using a variety of images of hypocrisy and vice. It shows the evil effects of 'enthusiasm' (a pejorative term in this period) on the human brain. It implies that the preacher is a Popish priest in disguise and the congregation is either insincere or wicked. For another Hogarth print on the same theme, see BMC 1785.

70. BMC 2432   Aug. 1739
This again suggests that Whitefield was both deceitful and associated with Catholicism. Methodism is shown as subversive and designed to mislead the ignorant.

71. BMC 3730   July 1760

Whitefield, the novelist Sterne and the playwright Foote are depicted as agreeing in their love of money. Whitefield had recently attacked Foote in the press. Whitefield, with his more flamboyant style and distinctive squint, appeared in prints much more frequently than Wesley.

72. BMC 4005   May 1763
    Another allegation that Methodist preachers are motivated by greed and that their congregations are lewd and disorderly.

73. BMC 4570 (c.1770)
An unusual, non-satirical and rather old-fashioned Methodist print, with a simple pious message.

The TREE of LIFE.

74. BMC 5495   1778
One of several attacks on John Wesley for alleged hypocrisy after his denunciation of the American rebels.

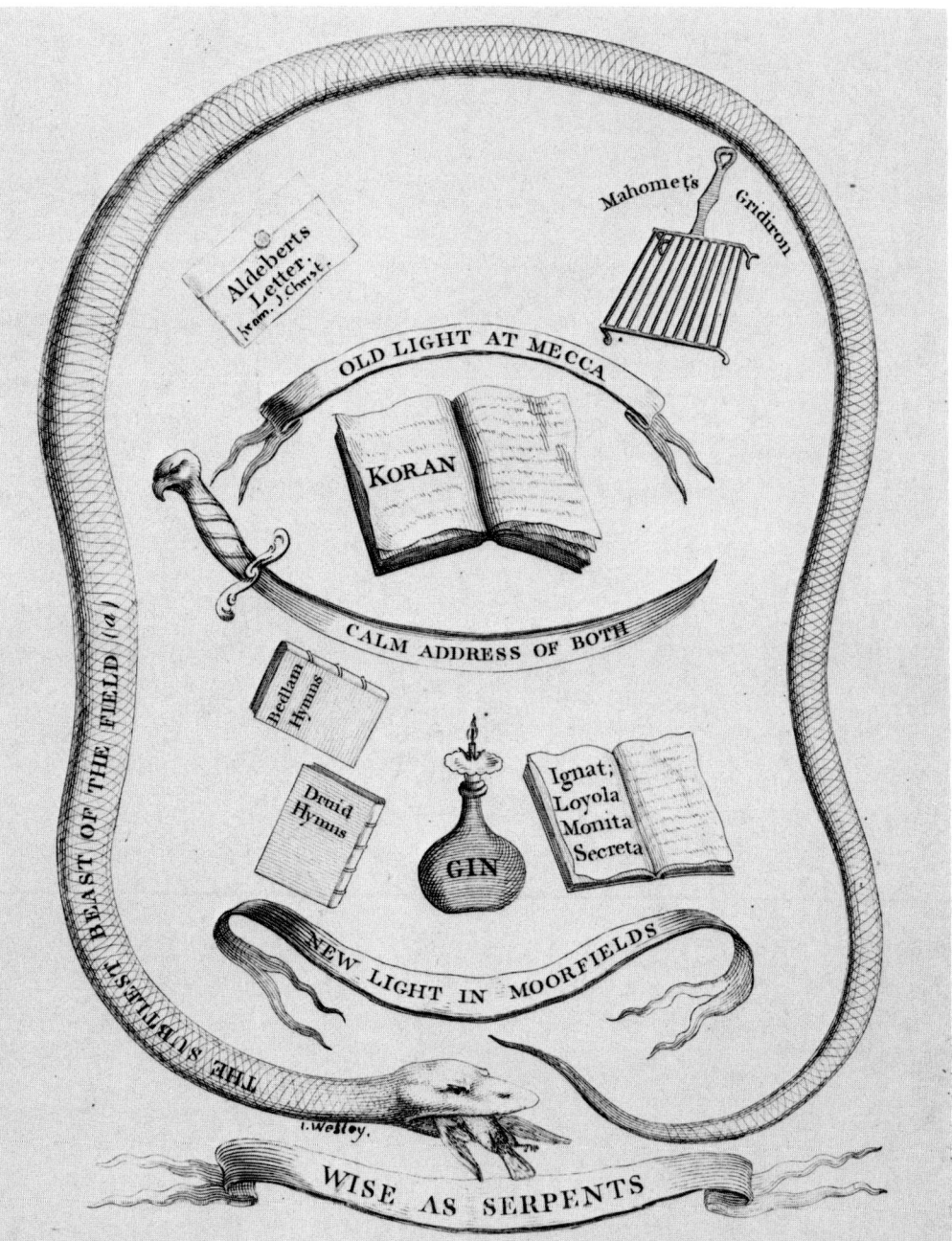

75. BMC 9818   (1801)
The Methodist preacher has by now become as much a standard figure of fun as the drunken parson.

76. BMC 1607   1717
    One of the processions organised by the Whigs to exploit anti-Catholicism and anti-Jacobitism. Note the warming pan in which (legend had it) a suppositious child had been smuggled into the queen's bedchamber in 1688, that child being passed off as James II's son, the Old Pretender.

F. *The Warming-pan, &c.* G. *The Champion in Armour.* H. *The Sans-Bell.* I. *Two Men sprinkling Holy Water.* K. *The Pope, the Devil, and the Pretender.*

L. *A Cardinal, Jesuit, and Fryer Cordelier.* M. *Three other Fryers and Confessors.* N. *A Royal Bearer carried by Four Men.*

A, B. *Generals Mar and Forster.* C. *The Pretender's Standard.* D. *A Drum Muffled.* E. *Six Scots Rebels in their Highland Dress as they enter'd London.*

77. BMC 2156   (1735)   Hogarth
This is unusual in satirising Catholic ritual and doctrine rather than the political implications of Catholicism.

Transubstantiation Satirized.

78. BMC 2636   Sept. 1745   C. Mosley
Produced at a time when the Young Pretender was making himself master of Scotland, this reproduces all the clichés of 'Popery and arbitrary government' and urges the English not to trust the Pretender's disavowals of persecution. See also BMC 2658, 2790.

The INVASION or
Perkins Triumph—
a Protestant Print.

Inscrib'd to all true-lovers of their Religion & Liberty.

79. BMC 2660   (1745)
Another print provoked by the '45, stressing the absurdity of certain Catholic practices and the Pretender's links with France.

80. BMC 2675   1745
A somewhat subtler print, which plays on prejudices against Catholicism and the Scots, but also satirises certain domestic weaknesses which reduce England's capacity to resist, notably the misuse of places and pensions and the idleness and selfishness of the Anglican clergy.

81. BMC 3446   March 1756   W. Hogarth
A typical, wartime anti-French cartoon stressing the poverty in which the French live (the consequence of Popery and absolutism) and the bloodthirstiness of the Catholic clergy.

82. BMC 5534   April 1779
This was inspired by the Scots' resistance to the 1778 Catholic Relief Act, which had provoked serious rioting in February. It treats the Scots with unusual sympathy: George III's minister Lord Bute had been the subject of some viciously anti-Scottish cartoons. Note the Beast of Revelation, yet again.

83. BMC 5643   Feb. 1780
A typical piece of Protestant Association propaganda, with the Catholic powers leagued to impose Catholicism on England and Scotland. The Anglican clergy are depicted, for once, as staunchly opposed to Popery.

84. BMC 5678   2 June 1780   (Gillray?)
George III is depicted as misled by Lord North into supporting the Relief Act and so promoting Popery, but the Papists' wiles are opposed by Gordon. This print was issued to coincide with the Protestant Association's great petition to Parliament.

Ecclesiastical, and, POLITICAL, state of the NATION.

85. BMC 5679   9 June 1780   Gillray
Published at the end of the Gordon Riots, it depicts anti-Popery as a mere pretext for plunder.

NO POPERY or NEWGATE REFORMER.

Tho' He says he's a Protestant, look at the Print,
The Face and the Bludgeon, will give you a hint,
Religion he cries, in hopes to deceive,
While his practice is only to burn and to thieve.

Publish'd as the Act Directs, June 5.t 1780 by J. Catch of St Giles's.

86. BMC 5680   10 June 1780
Published on the day of Gordon's arrest after the riots, George III is now shown favouring Popery.

A Great Man at his Private Devotion.

87. BMC 5685   June 1780   (Carey)
Imaginary scene in the Gordon Riots, with John Wesley urging on the crowd. Wesley had written to the press in support of the Protestant Association but was not involved in the riots.

Religious strife is raisd to life,　　FANATACISM REVIVED　　No Popery! be loud doth cry,
by canting whining Johns;　　　　　　　　　　　　　　　　　Ye the deluded throng

88. BMC 5841 (1781?)
A fictitious representation of the presentation of Gordon's petition. It seeks to show that the Protestant Association was a respectable and orderly body and alleges that the riots were fomented by emissaries of the Papists.

89. BMC 5844   July 1781   O'Neil
    The most accurate representation of the Gordon Riots.

An Exact Representation of the Burning, Plundering and Destruction of NEWGATE by the Rioters, on the memorable 7th of June 1780.

90. BMC 7209 1787
After his acquittal on a charge of treason, Gordon went to Amsterdam, but was deported. He settled in Birmingham, lived as a Jew and eventually became insane. 'Birmingham' meant counterfeit or inferior.

91. BMC 8536   (1794?)   Rowlandson
See also BMC 13115. Duke's Place was renowned as a Jewish quarter.

JEWS AT A LUNCHEON.
Or a peep into Duke's Place.

92. BMC 11113 (1808) Rowlandson

*Get Money, Money still,
And then let Virtue follow, if she will.*

93. BMC 3202   Nov. 1753
A print exulting in the repeal of the Jewish Naturalisation Act: Christian values have outweighed the power of bribery. Whitefield and Wesley both preached against the Act.

94. BMC 3204 (1753)
Again the accusation that Pelham and Newcastle had been bribed by the Jews to support the bill. It raises the bizarre spectre of the Jews taking over England if the bill remained law and the still more bizarre claim that the bill's ultimate objective was to bring in the Pretender.

A PROSPECT OF THE NEW JERUSALEM

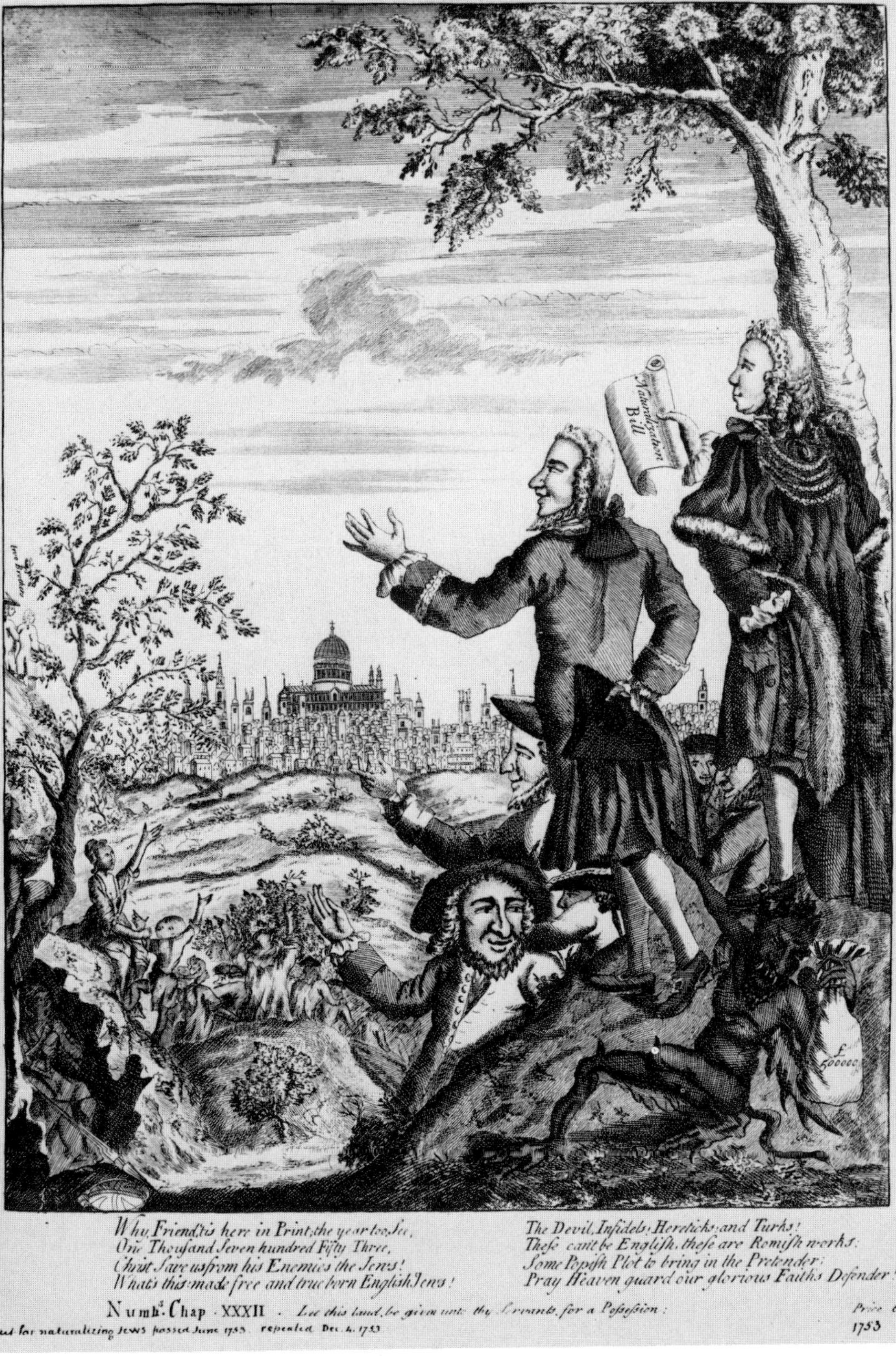

Why Friend, tis here in Print; the year too, see,
One Thousand Seven hundred Fifty Three,
Christ Save us from his Enemies the Jews!
What's this: made free and true born English Jews!

The Devil, Infidels; Hereticks; and Turks!
These can't be English, these are Romish works:
Some Popish Plot to bring in the Pretender;
Pray Heaven guard our glorious Faiths Defender!

Numb^s. Chap · XXXII · *Let this land, be given unto thy Servants, for a Possession:* *Price 6^d*

act for naturalizing JEWS passed June 1753 · repealed Dec. 4. 1753 · 1753

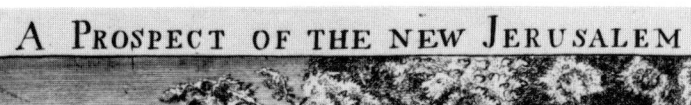

95. BMC 3208 (1753)
A third, more obviously anti-semitic print occasioned by the Jew Bill controversy.

96. BMC 7887   1 July 1791

From the *Attic Miscellany*. A distinguished chemist and Unitarian minister, Priestley was one of the most radical of the 'rational Dissenters'. He campaigned for the repeal of the Test and Corporation Acts and welcomed the French Revolution. This print appeared shortly before the riots occasioned by a dinner to celebrate the second anniversary of the storming of the Bastille. During the riots, Priestley's house and laboratory were destroyed. See also BMC 7636.

ATTIC MISCELLANY.
Political Portraiture   N.º 4.

DOCTER PHLOGISTON,
The PRIESTLEY politician or the
Political Priest.

97. BMC 7896   Aug. 1791
From *Bon Ton Magazine*. This shows, not the Priestley riots, but a village bonfire, organised by the squire, in which Priestley was burned in effigy after a mock trial.

98. BMC 11764   1811
This shows the London meeting house of Elias Carpenter, one of Joanna Southcott's followers. The congregation consists of ruffians and hypocrites and Carpenter sells tickets to Heaven, signed by the Angel Gabriel. This refers to Joanna's practice of giving 'seals' to the chosen. Some of her followers did make money out of the credulity of those who accepted her prophecies, but Joanna 'sealed' no-one after 1808, when one of her 'chosen' was convicted of murder.

INTERIOR VIEW OF THE HOUSE OF GOD.

99. BMC 12331   Sept. 1814   (Williams?)
Published in the last year of Joanna's life, this tells of a tradesman who played a trick on his wife to cure her of her belief in Joanna's prophecies. See also BMC 12334, 12336.

100. BMC 9240   Aug. 1798   Gillray
From the *Anti-Jacobin Magazine*. A wide-ranging satire linking English radicals (or radical sympathisers) with Larevellière-Lépeaux, one of the French Directory, and patron of the official republican religion of 'Théophilanthropie'. The radicals are shown as combining deceit with ignorance. Among those depicted are former staymaker Tom Paine (the crocodile in stays), Coleridge and Mary Wollstonecraft. For fuller details, see Stephens and George, *Catalogue*, VII. 468–72.

101. BMC 13274   Oct. 1819   G. Cruikshank
Richard Carlile, the freethinker, was prosecuted for blasphemous libel for republishing Paine's works. A combative character, he subpoena'd the Archbishop of Canterbury and questioned him about the truth of Christianity. The trial was promoted, not by the government, but by the Society for the Suppression of Vice, one of the private societies started by the Evangelicals. For the Society, see also *119*.

102. BMC 13347 'J.B.'
Published by Carlile, this is not only anti-clerical but hostile to all organised religion. It shows a parson and a Dissenting minister combining (for their own profit) to keep the people ignorant. For an earlier print on the same theme, see BMC 8030.

103. } BMC 13547–8   Jan. 1820   J. Baker
104. } From *The Christian House Built by Truth on a Rock*, an answer to William Hone's radical *Political House that Jack Built*. The central figure among the deists and atheists is Paine. The style is typical of the cheap polemical tracts of the period and shows conservative writers trying to match the radicals and to appeal to a poorer readership. See also George, *Caricature*, II. plate 72.

"Blessed are ye, when Men shall revile you and persecute you, and shall say all manner of Evil against you falsely, for my sake". V. Matt. II v. 5.

These are the Sage DOCTORS,
    Of Learning profound,
Consecrated to Virtue,
    And taught to expound
The Truths in those Volumes,
    Condemning each Vice,
Real Treasures of Value,
    And "Gems without Price";
That lay in the HOUSE,
    Built by Truth on a Rock,
Celebrious for Ages, above
    The rude shock
Of Infidel tempests, that
    Howl round its base,
Unable to strike any part
    Out of place,
Which increasing with years,
    Will appear more sublime,
Till the ray of its Glory,
    Enlightens each Clime.

104. BMC 13548 Jan. 1820 J. Baker
See *103*.

"Ye Serpents, ye generation of Vipers, how can ye escape the damnation of Hell?" XXIII St. Matthew, 33 ver.

These were ATHEISTS & DEISTS,
　　　　　A mushroom race!
Of virulent speech, and
　　　　　Their Country's disgrace!
Blind Sophists! who falsely
　　　　　Call'd Reason their guide:
Destroyers of Truth! who
　　　　　Could witless deride
Those excellent Doctors,
　　　　　Of Learning profound,
Consecrated to Virtue,
　　　　　And taught to expound
The Truth's in those Volumes, condemning each Vice,
Real Treasures of Value, & "Gems without Price",
That lay in the HOUSE, built by Truth on a Rock,
Celebrious for Ages, above the rude shock
Of Infidel tempests, that howl round its base,
Unable to strike any part out of place,
Which increasing with years, will appear more sublime,
Till the ray of its Glory, enlightens each Clime.

105. BMC 14815   (1825)   (T. Hood)
A satire on religious enthusiasts – Evangelicals and Sabbatarians – but also on enthusiasts of a very different kind – the political radicals, the 'march of mind' men and the founders of London University.

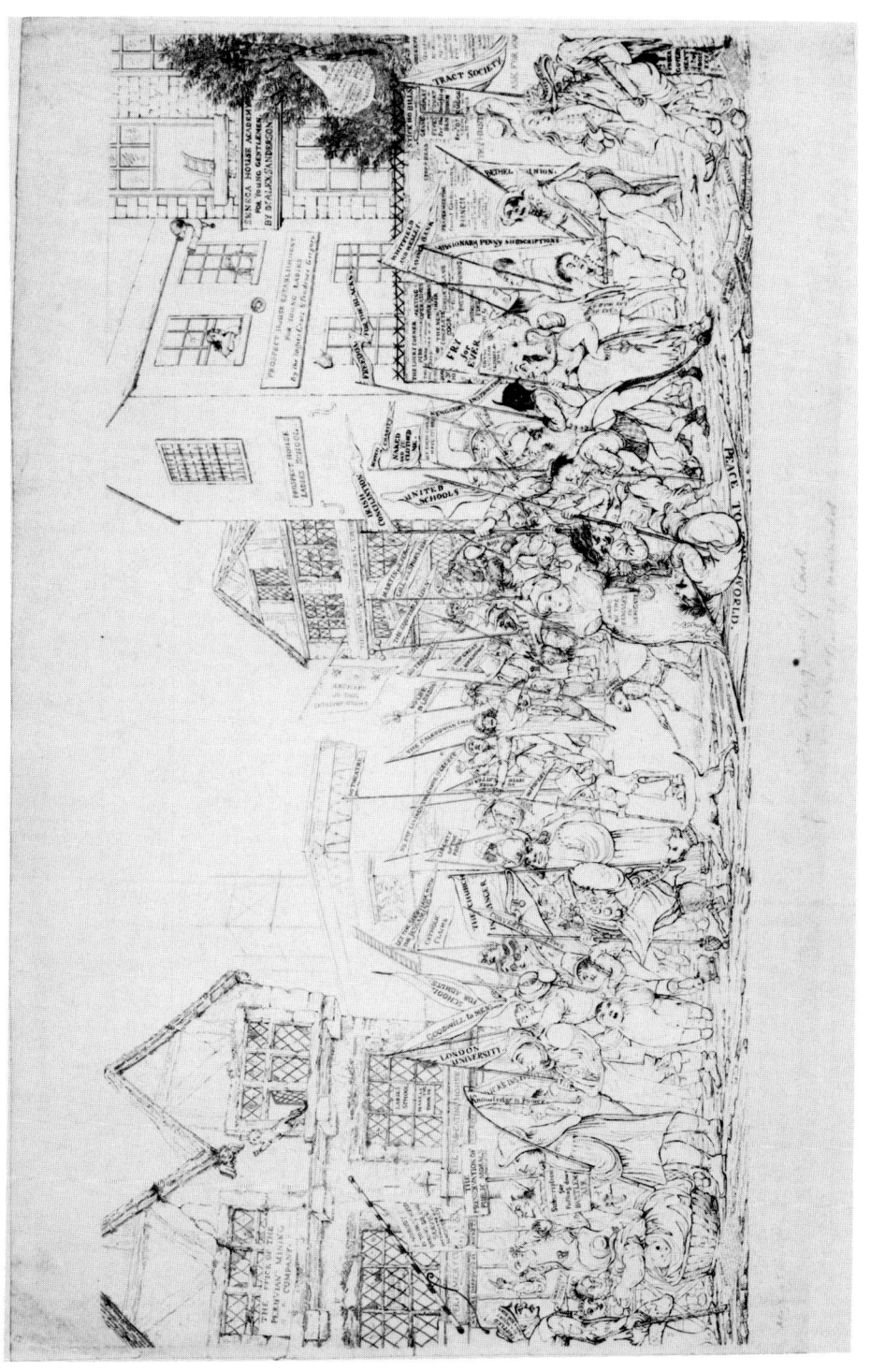

106. BMC 15889   Oct. 1829
A satire on religious beliefs of all kinds. Joanna Southcott talks of the 'Shiloh', the messiah she claimed to be carrying in 1814.

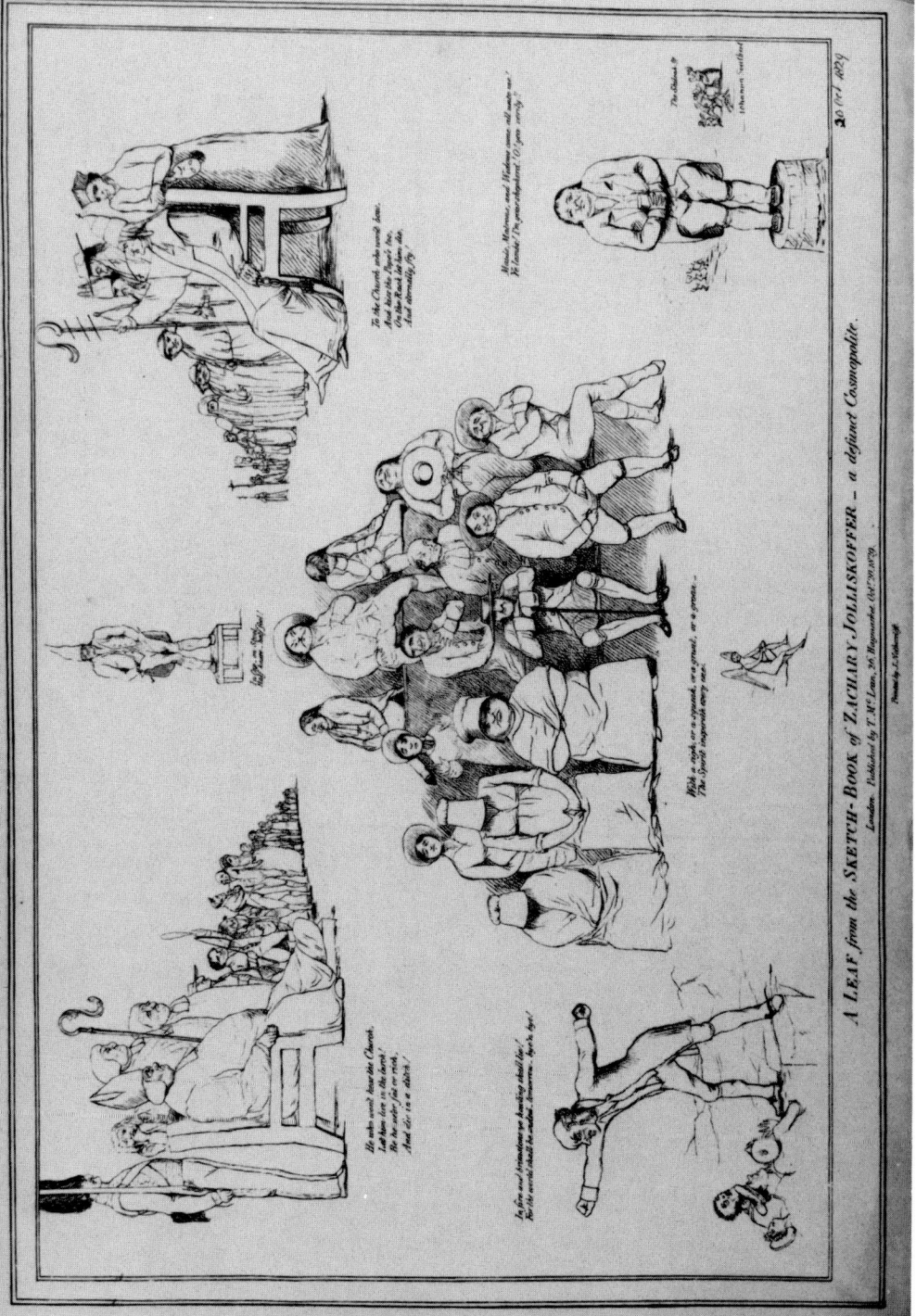

A LEAF from the SKETCH-BOOK of ZACHARY JOLLISKOFFER – a defunct Cosmopolite.

107. BMC 6209   April 1783   Gillray
A satire on the burden of tithe for both the country gentleman (an officer in the militia, not the army) and the poor farmer. Note the reference to 'popish canons': much of the canon law dated back to before the Reformation.

108. BMC 6737   1784
Typical satire on clerical greed. See also BMC 5800, 7778, 9138.

TYTHE IN KIND; OR THE SOW'S REVENGE.

109. BMC 8428   Feb. (1794?)
Such attacks on clerical gluttony are nothing new (see *60*). What *is* new is the strong element of social criticism in the comparison between the Archbishop and the Spitalfields weaver. See also BMC 8323.

110. BMC 8635   April 1795   I. Cruikshank
Shows the similarities between the opponents of reform in Church and state.

No REFORM, No REFORM.

111. BMC 13224   April 1819   G. Cruikshank
Another attack on clerical rapacity, occasioned by a bill to increase the stipends of certain London incumbents.

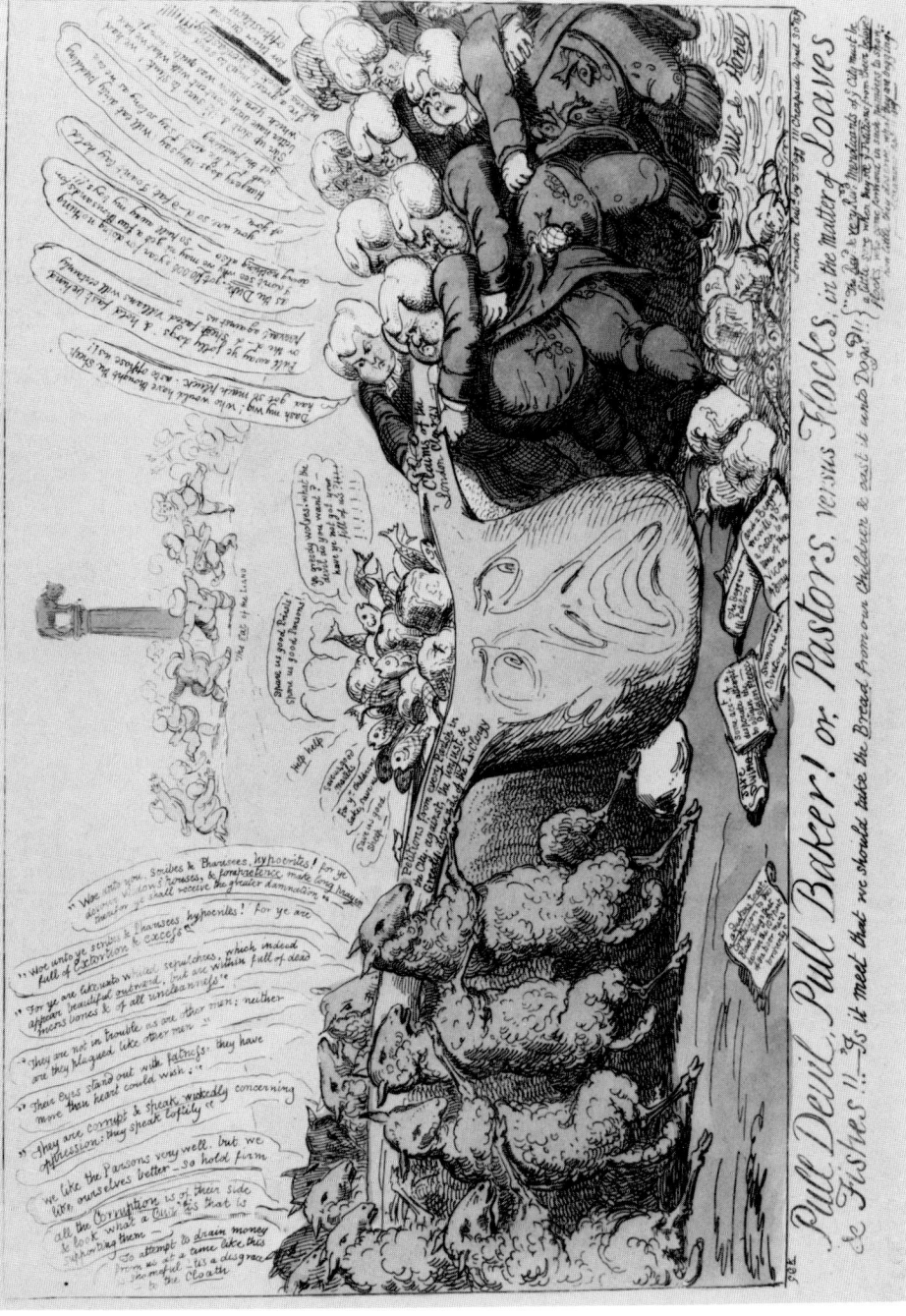

112. BMC 13281   Dec. 1819   G. Cruikshank
An attack on clerical magistrates, their conservatism and their failure to practise the Christian conduct which they preach. It refers especially to Charles Wicksted Ethelston, who read the Riot Act at Peterloo. Note the reference to the threat of military rule. See George, *Caricature*, II., plate 71a.

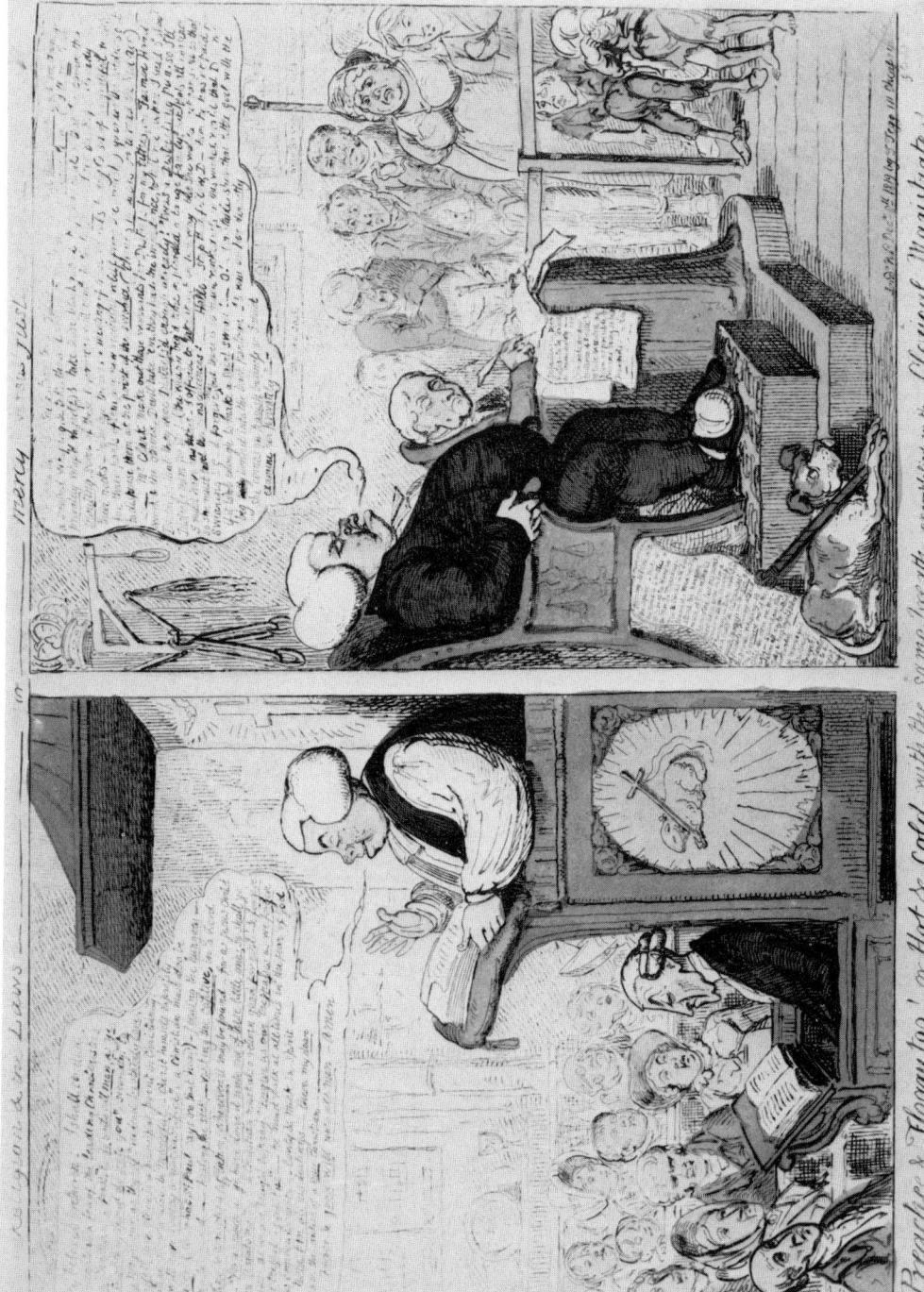

113. BMC 13288   Dec. 1819   G. Cruikshank
Shows the clergy as part of an oppressive and cripplingly expensive establishment (a theme much expounded by Cobbett), with a reference to the prospect of military rule. One parson holds the constable's staff – a clerical magistrate. The muzzle refers to the Blasphemous and Seditious Libels Act of 1819. See also BMC 9038, 13295, 15363.

Poor BULL & his Burden — or the Political MURRAION!!!
"And the land stank — so num'rous was the fry."
— What will become of these Vermin, if the Bull should Rise—?!!!!!!!!!!!

114. BMC 15543 (c. July 1828) Seymour
This illustrates the crumbling of public acceptance of the existing church establishment and political order in the later 1820s: they survive thanks to the penalties of law and the threat of force. From the *First Book for the Instruction of Students in the King's College*, a strongly secularist and anticlerical attack on King's in particular and the Church in general. Brougham, here pushing open the door to the universities, was a leading promoter of London University.

SUPPORTING CHURCH AND STATE.
"Labourers in the Wineyard"
First Book Instructions to students of Kings College 1829

115. BMC 15798   June 1829   T. Jones
A satire on the Church's wealth and pastoral failings.

The MAN WOT LOOKS ARTER the CHURCH—preferment.

For a Bishop must be blameless, as the Steward of God; not self-will'd, not soon angry, not given to WINE, no striker, not given to **Filthy Lucre**; But a lover of hospitality, a lover of good men; **SOBER, JUST, HOLY, TEMPERATE.** Titus, Ch. 1 V. 7 & 8.

<u>One</u> of the English Bishops income is £1300 pr. An^m <u>More</u> than 84 of the Archbishops & Bishops of France put together!

116. BMC 16592   March 1831
From *Maclean's Monthly Sheet of Caricatures*. This was inspired by a remark in Parliament that it was dangerous to tell the public that the curates performed their tasks better than the incumbents.

117. BMC 5107   March 1773
This refers to the Feathers Tavern petition, in which certain Cambridge dons and others, most of them with heterodox views, asked Parliament to be freed of the need to subscribe the Thirty-Nine Articles. The petition was rejected, as was a bill for the relief of Dissenters.

The Zealots for, & Against the true Religion.

118. BMC 12624   (1815/16)   G. Cruikshank
The two royal dukes of Kent and Sussex were involved with various Evangelical and Dissenting bodies of a moral and philanthropic nature. This involvement was exaggerated and depicted as support for Dissent and hostility to the Church.

119. BMC 12814   Nov. 1816   Williams
A satire on one aspect of the Evangelicals' concern for moral purification, the efforts of the Lord Mayor Wood to clear London's streets of prostitutes. All concerned are depicted as hypocrites. Note the paper referring to the Society for the Suppression of Vice (see *101*).

City Scavengers cleansing the London Streets of Impurities!!

120. BMC 13107 (1818)
A fairly typical contrast between the Dissenters' hell-fire preaching and the Anglican style, bland to the point of tedium. Cobbett noted that a sermon by the dean of Rochester was all 'general, commonplace, cold observation', while a nearby Methodist was obsessed with damnation: *Rural Rides*, I. 225, 232–3. See also BMC 9121–2, 9647.

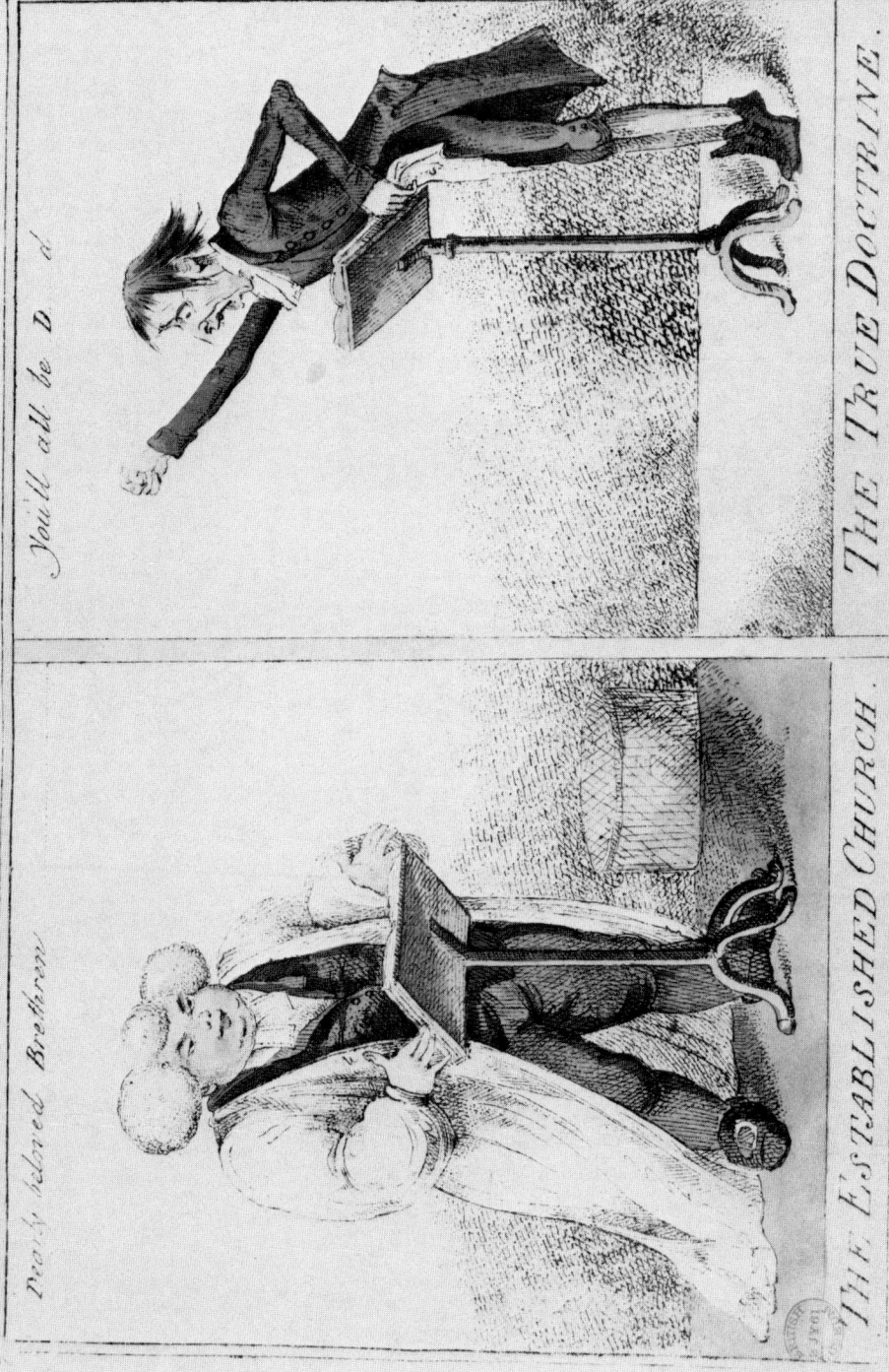

121. BMC 11745   Dec. 1811   Rowlandson
Bell was a leading critic of the British and Foreign School Society, founded by Lancaster (a Quaker) in 1808. His criticisms and those of other churchmen led to the founding of the National Society for Educating the Poor in the Principles of the Church (1811).

BELL and the DRAGON.

122. BMC 13276   Nov. 1819
An attack on Archbishop Manners-Sutton (for saying that the sixteenth-century Reformers preyed on popular ignorance) and on the National Society, using the old allegation that Anglicans were semi-Papists.

OLD THIRTY NINE shaking hands with his good Brother the Pope of Italy, or Covering up, versus Stealing up, the Bible.

123. BMC 14788   July 1825   R. Cruikshank
Lord Brougham and Jeremy Bentham played a major part in founding London University, now University College, a deliberate attempt to break the Church's monopoly of English university education. It was to teach no theology, a tradition maintained today.

The POLITICAL TOY-MAN.

124. BMC 15562 (c.Nov. 1828) Seymour

King's College was the Churchmen's reponse to 'godless' London University. For the time being (the print argues), money and influence may give King's the edge, but it is doomed (with the Church), for the intellectual superiority of Bentham (towering over the rest) will prevail.

KINGS COLLEGE VERSUS LONDON UNIVERSITY
or Which is the Weightiest

125. BMC 14644   April 1824   G. Cruikshank
All Souls', Langham Place was one of three churches designed by Nash for the Church Building Commissioners. It was much criticised and one M.P. declared himself ready to contribute to the cost of its demolition: see Port, *Six Hundred New Churches*, pp. 47–8.

NASHIONAL TASTE !!!
Dedicated without permission, to the Church Commissioners —

Providence sends meat,
The Devil sends cooks —

Parliament sends Funds —
But, who sends the Architects?—!!!

126. BMC 15536   (June 1828?)   'Paul Pry'
This follows an Act to abolish church briefs and provide for the better collection and use of voluntary contributions for church building and repairs. See also BMC 15559.

127. BMC 9183   March 1798   Gillray

A piece of propaganda aimed at the Catholic Irish. The government feared that the French might exploit Irish nationalism to provoke a strategically embarrassing revolt, so tried to appeal to Catholic resentment of the French government's maltreatment of the Catholic clergy.

128. BMC 11010   Aug. 1808   Gillray
A rare example of Catholic priests and nuns being treated sympathetically, because they are resisting the French.

SPANISH-PATRIOTS attacking the FRENCH-BANDITTI. — Loyal Britons lending a lift.

129. BMC 13009 (Dec. 1818) G. Cruikshank
A contrast to *128*. The Spaniards are no longer Britain's allies and the king has issued a decree against 'heretical and seditious' publications, providing an occasion for a traditional satire on 'popery and arbitrary government'.

130. BMC 13083   5 Nov. 1818   Marks

The burning of a 'Guy' on 5 November was a recent innovation; for its subsequent development and commercialisation, see H. Mayhew, *London Labour and the London Poor* (4 vols., London, 1861–2), III. 64–72. Previously the normal practice had been to have a simple bonfire or to burn an effigy of the pope.

A Genuine Dandy or Walking Guy. Nov. 5th 1818.

131. BMC 7628   (Feb.) 1790   J. Sayer
1790 saw the third attempt in three years to secure the repeal of the Test and Corporation Acts. As the repeal campaign was led by the radical Unitarians, Priestley and Price, who had welcomed the French Revolution, it was easy to argue that repeal would lead to the destruction of the established order in Church and state.

The REPEAL of the TEST ACT a Vision

132. BMC 7629   Feb. 1790   (Rowlandson?)
Similar to *131*. Price had preached a sermon, 'The Love of Our Country', to the Revolution Society, which had sent an address of congratulations to the French National Assembly. See also BMC 7630, 7635, 7686.

133. BMC 10403   May 1805   Rowlandson
One of several cartoons occasioned by an Irish emancipation petition. The Catholics offered to take the oath in the 1791 Act, but not the Test (which included a denial of transubstantiation). The petition was rejected by both Houses and the king was very hostile.

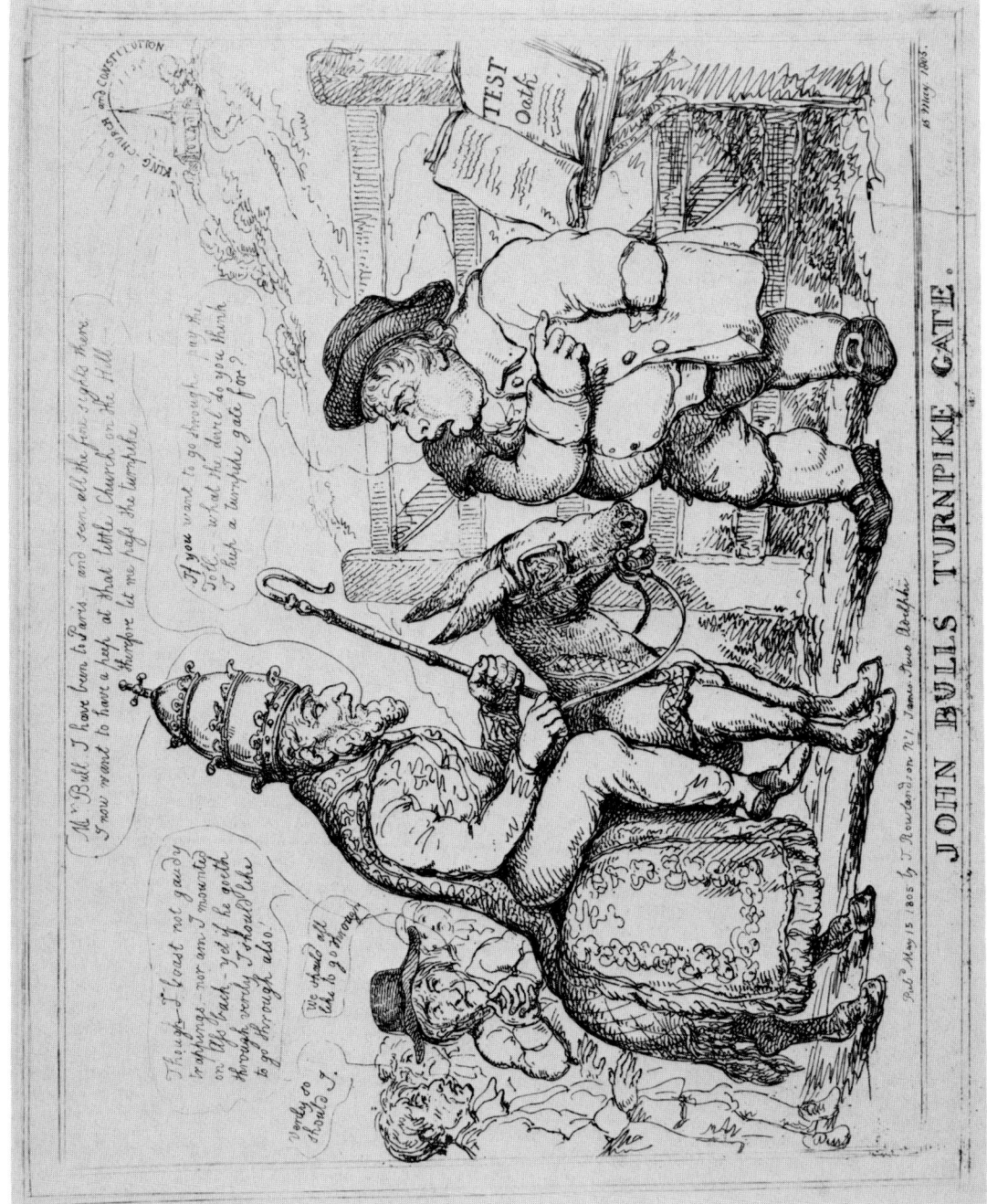

134. BMC 10404 May 1805 Gillray
On a similar theme to *133*. Note the link between the more radical Foxite Whigs, the republicans and the Catholics' demands. As in *131–2*, political radicals are seen as using a campaign for religious liberty to undermine the established order.

135. BMC 10405   May 1805   Gillray
Similar to *134*, but with more emphasis on the petitioners' links with France. Napoleon's conquest of Italy and control over the pope meant that Catholics could be seen as agents of the French as well as of the papacy.

136. BMC 10709   March 1807   Gillray
The Broad-bottom ministry (or Ministry of All the Talents) wished to open all ranks of the British and Irish armies to Catholics, whereas George III insisted on excluding them from the most senior ranks. The ministry resigned when George demanded a pledge to introduce no more pro-Catholic measures. See also BMC 10713–4.

137. BMC 12016   March 1813   G. Cruikshank
A bill to remove the civil and military disabilities of Catholics was withdrawn after a vote that they should remain excluded from Parliament. Note Napoleon riding on the pope's back.

The MERRY THOUGHT or; The CATHOLIC QUESTION Resolved.

138. BMC 14178   April/May 1821   Marks
Another Catholic emancipation bill passed the Commons but was rejected by the Lords. This print probably antedated the Lords' vote and is a typical parade of the horrors which would ensue if the Catholics gained the upper hand.

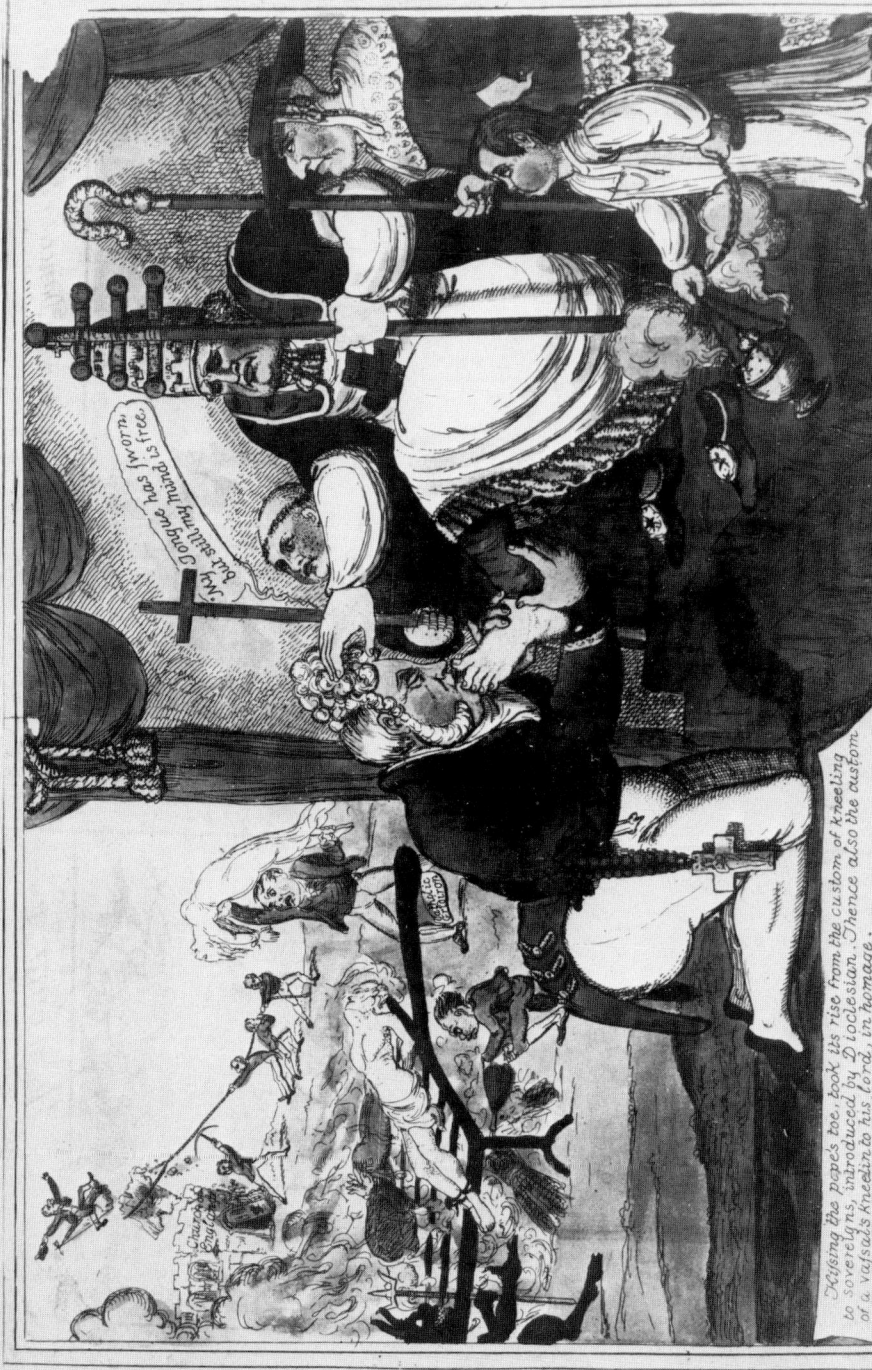

139. BMC 14179   May 1821   R. Cruikshank
Following the Lords' rejection of the emancipation bill, this shows the bill's leading opponents, Eldon and York, urged on by Wilberforce, Wellington and Liverpool. On the other side is Castlereagh, one of its supporters. See also BMC 14172.

POPE MISTAKEN;
"What ever is is not right."   anti Pope

140. BMC 14766   Feb. 1825   R. Cruikshank
O'Connell's Catholic Association gave the campaign for emancipation far more popular support, greatly strengthening the Catholics' bargaining power. Canning in fact favoured emancipation.

141. BMC 14771   May 1825   R. Cruikshank
Another illustration of the Duke of York's bitter opposition to emancipation. He declared that if he ever succeeded his brother, he would not assent to it.

142. BMC 15125 (1826) C. Perring
This depicts anti-Popery as a device of the ruling establishment to divert the people from considering their own wretched condition and the need for reform.

The "NO POPERY!" Cry.

COME Johnnies, come Jennies, come join,
　Join in the dance, and I'll tell;
Come Placemen, and Parsons, combine
　To make up the humbuging spell.
Join Pagan, Mahomet, and Jew;
　Join in the " No Popery !" cry,
We know not a word of its true,
　But—fudge, and its all my eye.

But now is the time for the trick,
　Make it up in perfection,
On Johnny we'll lay it on thick,
　At the forth-coming Election.
For ourselves its time to begin,
　And for seats to be carving,—
O, " Popery !"—*damnable* sin,
　Think of this whilst your starving

The cauldron, then let us now fill,
　For we have plenty to spare;
Add more fire,—pray dont let it chill,
　But all come in for their share.
For the City, a-*WARD* them a calf,
　Emblem of Old *BILLY'S* brains;
Why Johnny, what makes you to laugh,
　For you we are taking such pains.

Boroughmongers join in the rig,
　Join us Prosperity *FRED*;
Now throw in the *CHANCELLOR*'s wig,
　'Twill do as well as his *head*;
Of *Orange* let us have plenty,
　And dont be sparing of *PEEL*,
And *BANKS'S Heads*, tho' empty,
　Heads without brains cannot feel.

Let's put on some L—V—RP—L fire,
　For that will keep it a-light;
And deeds we'll perform that are dire,
　Fit for the shades of the night.
Come stir up the pot full of broth,
　And sing I diddle diddle ;
Come C—NN—G, thou mouth full of *froth*,
　A star upon the first fiddle.

A few of the *TENTH*—by the way,
　Drones like ourselves might be fed;
Our duty's to damn you to day,
　Their's to damn you after your dead.
Let's have a bit of *Johanna*,
　For she has left us her charms ;
'Twill serve us instead of manna,
　To keep up sectarian alarms.

Throw in the *Saints* altogether,
　And see that none of them stray,
For they'll fall out with each other,
　If you wont go to heaven their way.
Pure love it is makes them goad
　Your souls, they only regard,
They'll starve you to death on the road,
　That you may get your reward.

Come Grandames, if merry or not,
　At hearing old Grandames relate,
Bring all that you've heard to the pot,
　We'll make it a matter of state.
Bring Roasting and Broiling for grace,
　HOBGOBS and things that you dread;
We'll throw them, poor Johns, in your face,
　To fright you, like children, to bed.

JOHNNY you've got our protection,
　And pray keep alive your fears,
Keep up till past the Election,
　And then your nick'd for some years,
BURDETT, BROUGHAM, HUME, and such elves,
　With Freedom they may be cramm'd,
Who wish men to think for themselves,
　Such heresy, ought to be damn'd.

Independence, and honour dont mind,
　They're not the men for our boat ;
" No Popery" men, we want to find,
　Those who will squeak out a Vote,
Autonimons—let them be aye.
　One monysyl.—let them sing
To give us a aye or a nay
　Like puppets pull'd by a string

　Let such talents as those, be your choice,
　　And on them, safely repose,
　For they, with yourselves will rejoice,
　　While like they're led by the nose.
　Tho' I am selected, to prate,
　　'Tis no very dignified job ;—
　But fools, there must be in the state,
　　There must dear John—Help me God.

143. BMC 15366   March 1827   'H.H.' (Heath)
Shows the division in the cabinet, between Canning and Eldon, on the emancipation question.

144. BMC 15398   May 1827   R. Cruikshank
When Liverpool resigned because of illness, Canning was the obvious successor as prime minister. Several leading opponents of emancipation (Wellington, Eldon and Peel) resigned. Canning died in August.

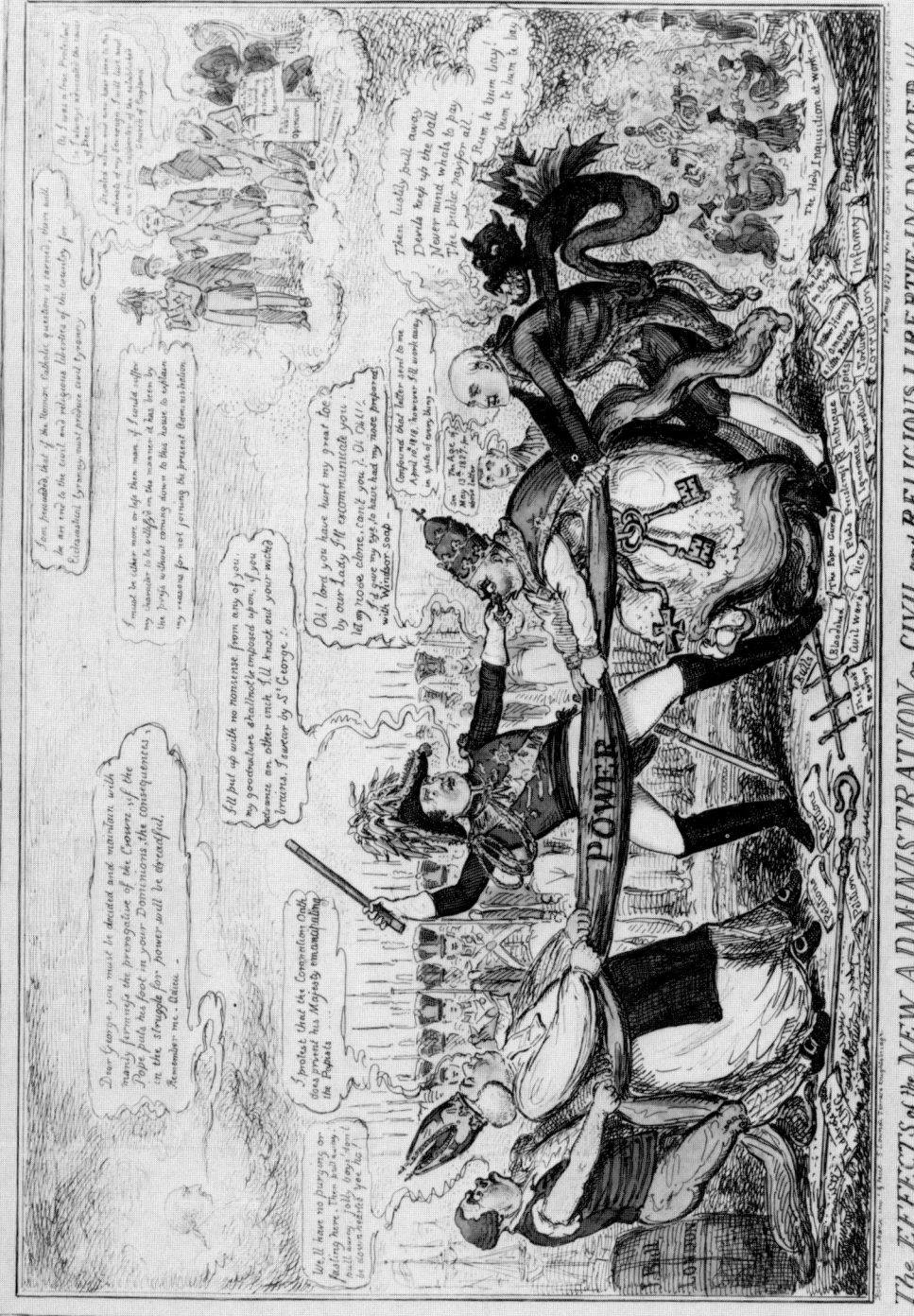

145. BMC 15661 (c.Feb. 1829) Heath
Less overtly political than *142*, this suggests that the popular hostility to Catholicism owed much to ignorance and misinformation.

146. BMC 15677   March 1829   (Seymour?)
Wellington and Peel have come to accept the need for emancipation, but a majority of peers are still hostile and have mobilised public opinion against it.

The Mountain in Labour — or Much ado about nothing.

147. BMC 15690   March 1829   (R. Cruikshank?)
A pessimistic response to the passing of emancipation, alleging that it meant the end of the existing constitution and of the Protestant religion. See also BMC 15701.

148. BMC 15713 (April) 1829 Seymour/Olivatte
A rather complicated depiction of the battle between toleration and prejudice. Wellington and various Whig and radical supporters of emancipation do battle with Eldon. Past supporters of toleration include such unlikely figures as Henry VIII and Charles I.

149. BMC 15819   June 1829   (Seymour?)
After the repeal of the Test and Corporation Acts and the passing of emancipation, Churchmen felt betrayed by their lay allies (notably Wellington and Peel), but showed little inclination to reform the Church.

150. BMC 16706   June 1831   Seymour
From *Maclean's Monthly Sheet*. The Tory ministry, desperate to survive the storm created by the demand for parliamentary reform, has conceded emancipation. Wellington refuses to concede any more.

151. BMC 16798   Oct. 1831   'H.B.'
This refers to the violent reaction to the Lords' rejection of the Reform Bill. Wellington's windows were smashed and several bishops were insulted or assaulted.

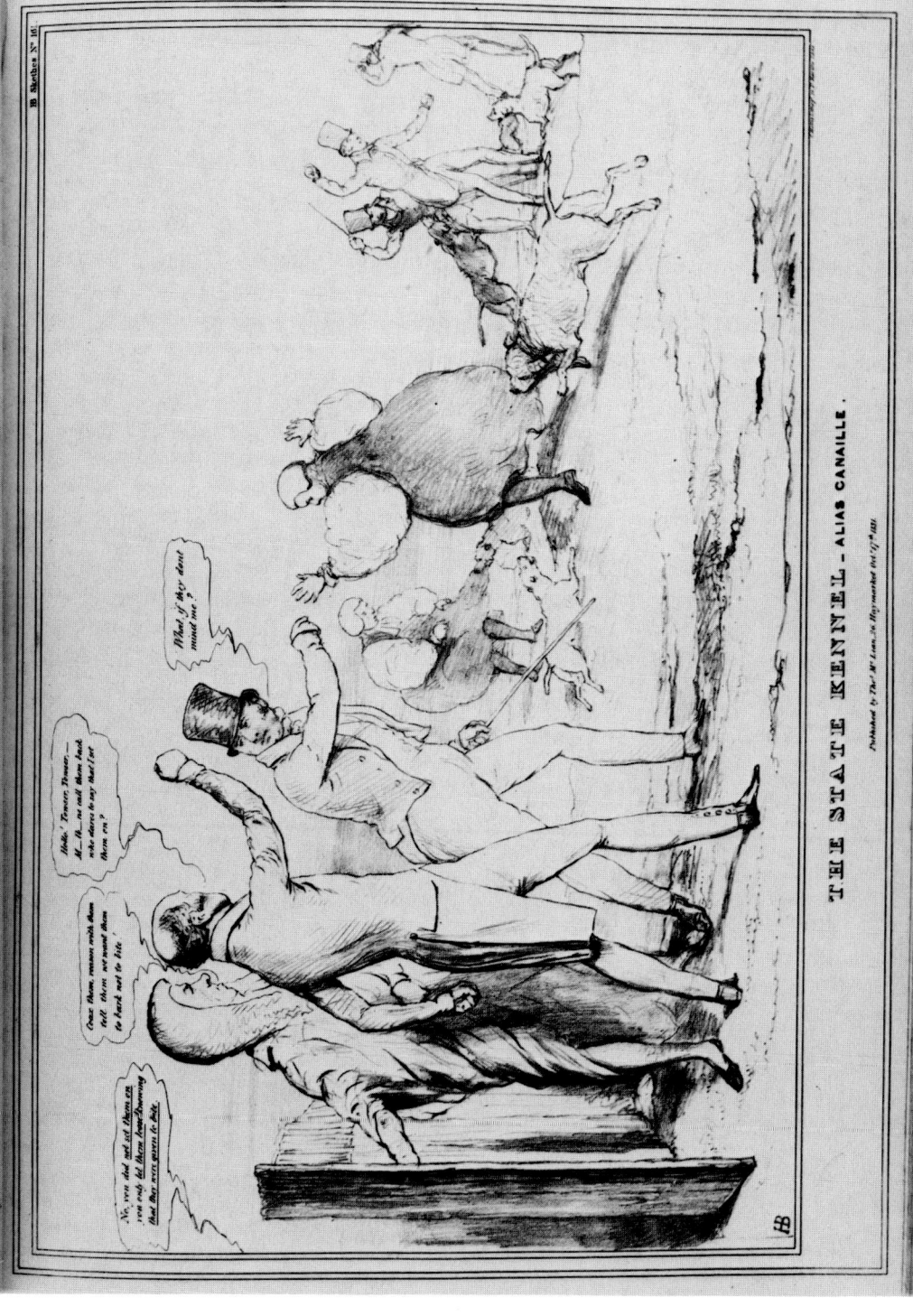

152. BMC 16808   Nov. 1831   Seymour

From *Maclean's Monthly Sheet*. The bishops were particularly blamed for the failure of the Reform Bill. Lord Grey, its promoter, was far from displeased at their unpopularity.

"THE FRY-ER OF ORDERS GREY"

153. BMC 17165   July 1832   Seymour
From *Maclean's Monthly Sheet*. This suggests that the Reform Bill (now passed) will lead to the total dissolution of the old order in Church and state and that it is not a 'final measure', as the Whigs claim.

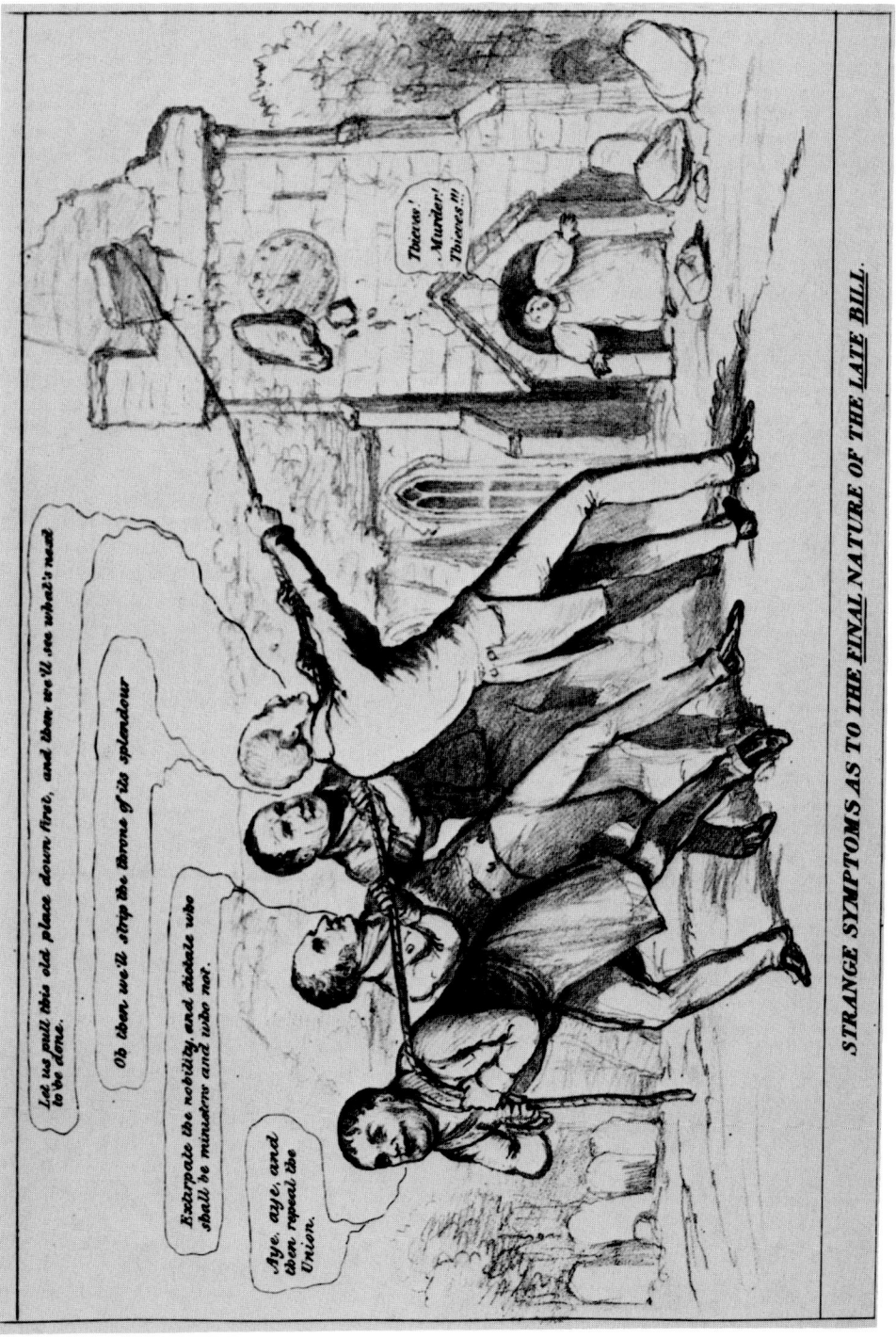

STRANGE SYMPTOMS AS TO THE FINAL NATURE OF THE LATE BILL.

154. BMC 17286   Nov. 1832   Seymour
From *Maclean's Monthly Sheet*. A comment on the press campaign (greatly aided by the Extraordinary Black Book) against the corruptions and anomalies in the distribution of Church preferments.